JOHN BELL HOOD:
EXTRACTING TRUTH
FROM HISTORY

JOHN BELL HOOD:
EXTRACTING TRUTH
FROM HISTORY

Thomas J. Brown

Library of Congress Control Number: 2012916554
ISBN: Hardcover   978-1-4797-1324-0
                 Softcover   978-1-4797-1323-3
                 Ebook   978-1-4797-1325-7

To order additional copies of this book, contact:
Xlibris Corporation
1-888-795-4274
www.Xlibris.com
Orders@Xlibris.com
116303

CONTENTS

Abstract

JOHN BELL HOOD
EXTRACTING TRUTH FROM HISTORY

Thomas J. Brown

The year 2011 brings us the sesquicentennial celebration of the American Civil War. Surprisingly, 150 years later, students continue to find themselves asking many of the same questions about the great national tragedy faced during the centennial in 1961. For example, did slavery cause the great conflict, or did constitutional questions act as the catalyst? Does the Battle of Gettysburg represent *the* turning point of the War, or did that occur elsewhere?

In connection with the last question, Lost Cause advocates, those great pro-Confederacy propagandists, found convenient villains to blame for the Southern defeat. One of these, Confederate General John Bell Hood, plays an important role. This paper contends that in his case, the Lost Cause is wrong and that Hood's historical treatment has been false.

Standard critical treatment of John Bell Hood over the years has tended to characterize the general as rash, overaggressive, and lacking in strategic imagination. For such critical historians, Hood appears as old-fashioned and someone limited logistically to the frontal assault. These accounts mainly stress his negative aspects as a soldier and tend to center around the Battle of Franklin. This thesis, by analyzing every battle that Hood commanded as a leader of the Army of Tennessee, particularly those fought around Atlanta, reveals him to have been a far more bold, imaginative, and complex leader than has previously been portrayed.

ACKNOWLEDGMENTS

I would first like to thank my dedicated thesis advisor, Dr. Libra Hilde, for her immeasurable help and support throughout the process of this paper. I am also appreciative of my two other committee members, Professors Mary Pickering and Jeffrey Hummel, for their timely work in evaluating my paper. Many thanks to my good friend Sam Hood of West Virginia for guiding me to excellent sources, corresponding regularly, and sharing with me his knowledge and respect of his distant cousin John Bell Hood. Dr. Brandon Beck, retired professor from Shenandoah University, provided me with his military expertise and overall knowledge of Civil War events. I extend sincere gratitude to my friends and fellow brothers in the Sons of Union Veterans of the Civil War, especially Bob Nelson, for donating to me several excellent books from his precious collection, most notably a beautiful set of the Battles and Leaders series.

Last but not least, I must acknowledge my supportive family and friends who have endured this lengthy journey with me. Lots of love to my mother and father, Yvonne and Ed Brown, and my wife, Kathryn, for the countless hours she spent typing and editing my "masterpiece."

I am thankful for Dr. Amy Lin and her staff at UCSF who have monitored my health situation these past two years and made it possible for me to continue my educational program. Dr. Thomas Bradley and the staff of Community Hospital of the Monterey Peninsula also receive my deepest thanks.

INTRODUCTION

Historical Trauma

The standard portrait of Confederate General John Bell Hood created by historians reveals an emotionally troubled, overaggressive, careless man possessing little regard for the welfare of his soldiers. Historical writer Wiley Sword, for instance, labels Hood "a fool with a license to kill his own troops."[1] The Battle at Franklin, Tennessee, November 30, 1864, is examined in detail in this paper. Historian Thomas Robson Hay called it "an unnecessary and bloody fight, waged in an effort to make up for the hesitation the day before at Spring Hill."[2] Certainly, Franklin stands as one of the bloodiest assaults of the war; nearly two thousand Confederates died, but its necessity is debatable. This battle is positioned at the center of all controversies surrounding General Hood. Franklin represented the end result of three attempts by Hood to corner a twenty-thousand-man Union army commanded by James Schofield and prevent it from joining a greater force being assembled by General George H. Thomas at Nashville. Historian Winston Groom writes that "from Hood's perspective . . . the elusive Schofield was there in plain sight—a desperate plan for desperate times."[3] The argument presented in this thesis contends that Hood's frontal assault, far from being wild or careless, stood as an impetus of a massed charge—if the attackers could get close enough to a defensive position—often tended to dislodge the defenders.[4]

Historian Stanley F. Horn accuses Hood of lashing "out viciously at his subordinates, placing blame everywhere but where it belonged—himself."[5] As this study will show, Hood had good reason for being angry with some of his officers

---

[1] Wiley Sword, *The Confederacy's Last Hurrah: Spring Hill, Franklin and Nashville* (Lawrence: University Press of Kansas, 1992), 263.

[2] Thomas Robson Hay, *Hood's Tennessee Campaign* (Dayton, Ohio: Morningside Bookshop, 1976), 130. Hay's work was originally published as an essay in 1920.

[3] Winston Groom, *Shrouds of Glory: From Atlanta to Nashville: The Last Great Campaign of the Civil War* (New York: Grove Press, 1995), 218.

[4] Groom, *Shrouds of Glory*, 218.

[5] Stanley F. Horn, *The Army of Tennessee* (Norman: University of Oklahoma Press, 1953), 394.

following failure at Spring Hill, but he also accepted responsibility. In a letter of resignation addressed to the troops at Tupelo, Mississippi, on January 23, 1865, in reference to the Tennessee Campaign, Hood stated, "I am alone responsible for its conception."[6] Finally, in his memoirs, Hood declared plainly, "I failed utterly to bring on battle at Spring Hill."[7]

Hood's acceptance of blame for the entire campaign is generous. While the original conception may have been his, Confederate President Jefferson Davis, Secretary of War James Seddon, and General Beauregard endorsed the plan. Hood could no more have carried out the campaign without their approval than could Sherman have undertaken the March to the Sea without the approbation of President Lincoln, Secretary of War Edwin Stanton, and General Ulysses S. Grant.

Another common assertion is made by Horn when he states that in deciding upon the assault at Franklin, "Hood was consumed with . . . burning impetuosity" and further that "he could not wait . . . long enough to make further preparations."[8] As stated above, Franklin represented Hood's final opportunity to negate Schofield's force. With daylight fast disappearing and Union troops already moving across the Harpeth River toward Nashville, he could not afford to wait for his third corps. It would have arrived after dark, and placing artillery under those conditions would have been problematic and time-consuming. By daylight, as Hood knew, Schofield would have been gone.

Historian Thomas Connelly condemns Hood's aggressiveness, commenting that he arrived in the western theater with a "reputation as a reckless individual."[9] Connelly adds that Hood's impetuosity developed with success enjoyed while in Lee's army in Virginia and critically that "he had not abandoned his love of aggressive tactics" by 1864. Taking this further, he also accuses Hood of being a borderline "psychotic" who "associated valor with casualty figures."[10]

As will be discussed, historians Grady McWhiney and Perry Jamison argue persuasively that such aggressiveness was a common characteristic of Confederate officers and, moreover, that "Southerners, imprisoned in a culture that rejected careful calculation and patience, often refused to learn from their mistakes."[11]

---

[6]   *The War of the Rebellion: A Compilation of the Official Records of the Union and Confederate Armies*, Series I, Vol. XLV, part 1 (Washington: Government Printing Office, 1880), 805. Note: Hereafter cited as OR.

[7]   Lieutenant General John Bell Hood, *Advance and Retreat* (Edison: Blue and Gray Press, 1985), 287.

[8]   Horn, *The Army of Tennessee*, 398.

[9]   Thomas L. Connely, *The Army of Tennessee 1862-1865* (Baton Rouge: Louisiana State University Press, 1971), 431.

[10]   Ibid.

[11]   Grady McWhiney and Perry D. Jamieson, *Attack and Die: Civil War Military Tactics and the Southern Heritage* (Tuscaloosa: University of Alabama Press, 1982), Preface, xv.

Thus, Hood, far from being unusual, actually reflected the culture of his region. In short, Southerners during the antebellum and Civil War years indulged in defensive-aggressive feelings toward the North, which they regarded as a threat to their way of life.

Historian James Lee McDonough not only echoed his former professor, Thomas Connelly, but imitated a technique employed by Wiley Sword using strings of anti-Hood quotations while providing little or no balancing material.[12] By the 1990s, many historians had a ready-made agenda regarding John Bell Hood to portray him as an amateurish, near-psychotic incompetent who needlessly sacrificed the lives of his men. The blueprint for Hood's character and historical treatment, drawn upon by many historians, can be traced directly to Lost Cause—inspired writings within the *Southern Historical Society Papers*.

Wiley Sword's work, *The Confederacy's Last Hurrah*, winner of the 1992 Fletcher-Pratt Award, is the most virulent example of how words and partial quotations have been skillfully manipulated to create a misleading image of General Hood. In effect, Sword's book represents a compendium of false history repeated and layered upon itself over time. It is for this reason that an examination of examples from the book will be undertaken here.

In his first description of Hood, and probably the best example of how words and partial quotations have been manipulated to present a false image of Hood, Sword uses these words: "He looked like some backwoods lumberjack masquerading in the uniform of a Confederate general."[13] The title of the chapter itself, "A Cupid on Crutches," is demeaning.[14] Sword next created an image of the general's appearance, "a full beard and heavy mustache so elongated his face as to make it appear outlandish in size."[15] He continued by paraphrasing Mary Chesnut in *A Diary from Dixie:* "He had the look of an old crusader, something out of Don Quixote."[16] Sword wrote that in Chesnut's words, Hood's appearance suggested "awkward strength."[17] On the following page, Sword makes his first reference to Hood's supposedly deficient intellectual capacity. He "appeared to be . . . simplistic in his thinking and was not regarded as having a refined or calculating mind."[18] Sword failed to mention, however, which contemporaries regarded him in this way

---

[12]   James Lee McDonough, *Nashville: The Western Confederacy's Final Gamble* (Knoxville: University of Tennessee Press, 2004), 22.

[13]   Sword, *The Confederacy's Last Hurrah*, 6.

[14]   Ibid.

[15]   Sword, *The Confederacy's Last Hurrah*, 6.

[16]   Ibid.

[17]   Ibid.

[18]   Ibid., 7.

and went on in attempt to bolster his assertions by referring to Hood's "bare-bones high school equivalency."[19]

An analysis of these descriptions is instructive. To begin, a look at what Mary Chesnut actually said is revealing. This marked the first time that the famous diarist met young John Bell Hood, and she prefaced what would be quoted by saying that he had only recently been promoted from the rank of colonel to brigadier at the request of "Stonewall" Jackson, something Sword failed to mention. "When he came with his sad face—the face of an old crusader who believed in his cause—his cross and his crown—we were not prepared for that type of beau ideal of wild Texans," Chesnut commented. She continued, "He is tall, thin, shy with blue eyes and light hair, a tawny beard and a vast amount of it covering the lower part of his face . . . . He wears an appearance of awkward strength."[20]

The considerable space between Chesnut's actual words, the context within which they were used, and Sword's paraphrasing reveal his bias. Skillful orchestration of vocabulary and sentence structure show deliberate attempts to present a Bunyonesque character, strong and stupid, impressive in appearance but empty in mind. If one believes Sword's description, Hood was huge and burly, yet Chesnut used the term "thin." Chesnut was there, Sword was not. Moreover, Lieutenant Colonel Arthur Fremantle of Her Majesty's Cold Stream Guards visited the South as an observer during the war. He described Hood in their first meeting, "I was introduced to General Hood this morning; he is a tall, thin, wiry-looking man with a grave face and a light-colored beard, thirty-three years old, and accounted one of the most promising officers in the army."[21] The account of a North Carolina newspaperman who saw Hood following his recovery from losing a leg at Chickamauga also serves as contrast. "His personal appearance," the reporter commented, "like that of many other men of signal bravery." It was the very opposite "of the conventional idea of a fire-eater . . . . Somewhat bleached by illness rendering his delicate features more delicate with soft hair of light brown and beard nearly golden, he looks a mild, sensitive, and amiable man."[22]

Sword associated Hood with Don Quixote, a foolish character who went about tilting at windmills during the seventeenth century. A reader familiar with that tale will make a rather uncomplimentary association. Sword relied on the description given by Mary Chesnut, yet she never made any mention of the character from Cervantes's novel. Sword uses the word "simplistic" in reference to Hood's thinking processes

19   Ibid.
20   Mary Chesnut, *A Diary from Dixie* (Boston: Houghton Mifflin, 1949), 297.
21   Lieutenant Colonel Arthur T. L. Fremantle, *Three Months in the Southern States-April to June 1863* (Lincoln: University of Nebraska, 1991), 242.
22   Glen Tucker, *Chickamauga-Bloody Battle in the West* (Dayton: Morningside, 1992), 280. Tucker's notes on page 416 show the quotation coming from the Wilmington, North Carolina *Journal*, dated November 19, 1863.

throughout the book, and his reference to Hood's "bare-bones [education of] high school equivalency" reinforces the contention that Hood lacked intellectual ability. High school level education, however, was fairly common during the antebellum years, especially in the South. Indeed, such illustrious figures as Andrew Jackson, Zachary Taylor, and even Abraham Lincoln come readily to mind. Moreover, one of the Confederacy's most highly regarded generals, Nathan Bedford Forrest, had limited exposure to formal education during his formative years in rural Tennessee and Mississippi.[23] In the case of the first three, enemies regularly disparaged their mental abilities. Hood's "awkward strength" probably reflected his youth and recent promotion to the rank of brigadier general. He had not had time to accustom himself to the weight of new responsibilities. In fact, Hood's promotions came in rapid succession; within less than a year, he advanced from a lowly first lieutenant supervising artillery to a brigadier general in command of a brigade that became the most famous in Lee's army of Northern Virginia. Hood remembered the promotion as unexpected: "On the 7th of March, 1862, I followed up the movement with my regiment back in the direction of Fredericksburg; en route, and greatly to my surprise, I received information of my appointment as brigadier general and my assignment to the command of the Texas brigade."[24]

In reference to his time with the Army of Tennessee, Sword argued that Hood's men resented and even hated him. He did replace the popular Johnston under circumstances, which many perceived as political due to President Davis's prominent role. Another factor may have been the men of the western army viewed Hood as an interloper having served most of his time with Lee's army. Others, however, felt differently. Sam Watkins, who served with the Army of Tennessee at Chickamauga and Franklin, remembered Hood as "a noble, brave, and good man [whom] . . . we loved for his many virtues and goodness of heart."[25] Colonel Virgil S. Murphy of the 17th Alabama commented that "our government . . . placed Hood in command, and . . . I yielded to him my confidence and cordial cooperation."[26] Sergeant S. A. Cunningham of the 41st Tennessee, who served with Hood from Atlanta to Nashville, put the matter into perspective stating that "the removal of General Johnston and the appointment of Hood to succeed him . . . was an astounding event. So devoted to Johnston were his men that the presence and command of General Robert E. Lee would not have been accepted without complaint."[27]

---

23   Brain Steel Wills, *A Battle from the Start: The Life of Nathan Bedford Forrest* (New York: Harper Collins, 1992), 11-12.

24   Hood, *Advance and Retreat*, 20.

25   Sam Watkins, *Company Aytch* (New York: Penguin Putnam, 1989), 210.

26   Virgil Murphy: Diary in Southern Historical Collection, UNC at Chapel Hill. The diary has no page numbers.

27   *Confederate Veteran Magazine*, April, 1893.

In his harsh criticism of Hood's actions at Franklin, Sword makes personal attacks, stating that Hood was a "disabled personality prone to miscalculations and misperceptions. Unfortunately, he was also a fool with a license to kill his own men."[28] Sword took on the role of psychiatrist with biased supporting evidence. Some who witnessed events offered contrasting views to the sources Sword chose to keep. Sergeant-Major S. A. Cunningham remarked, "It was all important [for Hood] to act, if at all, at once."[29] Moreover, L. A. Simmons, who served with the 84th Illinois, wrote of Franklin in 1866, "In speaking of this battle, very many are inclined to wonder at the terrible pertinacity of General Hood in dashing column after column with such tremendous force . . . upon our center involving their decimation . . . . Yet this we have considered a most brilliant design and the brightest record of his generalship . . . he was playing a stupendous game for enormous stakes. Could he have succeeded in breaking the center, our whole army was at his mercy."[30] Wiley Sword avoided these quotations. His opinion of Hood can be neatly summarized in remarks made by Captain Sam Foster of the 24th Texas. "The wails and cries of widows and orphans made at Franklin . . . will heat up the fires of the bottomless pit to burn the soul of General J. B. Hood for murdering their husbands and fathers . . . . It can't be called anything else but cold-blooded murder."[31] While it is possible to trade positive and negative quotations in armies throughout history, there have been soldiers who liked their commanding general and those who did not, and both sides have not been shy about expressing their opinions.

Perhaps the most ringing endorsement came from former Tennessee Governor Isham Harris in a letter to President Jefferson Davis, dated Christmas Day 1865. "I have been with General Hood from the beginning of the [Tennessee] campaign and beg to say, disastrous as it has ended, I am not able to see anything that General Hood has done that he should not." Harris insisted, "Indeed, the more that I have seen and known of him . . . the more I have been pleased with him and regret to say that if all had performed their parts as he, the results would have been very different."[32] Harris's "if all" refers to failings of subordinate commanders at Spring Hill which will be discussed in chapter 3.

Wiley Sword has not been unique in his criticisms, although his have been the most harsh and deliberate. As noted above, his book serves as a collection of

[28]   Sword, *The Confederacy's Last Hurrah*, 263.

[29]   John Simpson, ed., *Reminiscence of the 41st Tennessee: The Civil War in the West* (Shippensburg, Pennsylvania: White Mane Books, 2001), 262.

[30]   L. A. Simmons, *The History of the 84th Illinois Volunteers.*

[31]   Eric Jacobsen, *For Cause and Country: A Study of the Affair at Spring Hill and Franklin* (Franklin: O'More Publishing Company, 2006), 438. Taken from Norman D. Brown, ed., one of Cleburne's Command: *The Civil War Reminiscences and Diary of Capt. Samuel T. Foster, Granbury's Texas Brigade, CSA* (Austin: 1980), 151.

[32]   OR, Vol. 45:2:732.

censures that have accumulated over the years. Such disparagement has become a mantra for discussions about General Hood. Selective referencing and hyperbole undermine a historian's credibility and mislead those who desire to learn about the past. As nineteenth-century German historian Leopold von Ranke once said, we must strive to tell the story: *Wie es eigentlich gewesen ist.*

Taken in its entirety, the military career of General Hood, although it ended badly, is marked more by success than failure. Sergeant Major Cunningham commented that "we regarded him [Hood] as a brave and daring soldier and an able division and corps commander but lacking in ability and experience as an army commander. Many, we know, will disagree with us, but we think to calmly and impartially view Hood's course we will be forced to accord to him abilities of the highest order."[33] His larger accomplishments are often overlooked because historians frequently conflate the final six months of Hood's service to the Confederacy as representative of the whole. That Hood qualified to command an entire army is not argued here but that he possessed exceptional ability at brigade and divisional levels is. Because of officer shortages due to high casualty levels, Hood, like many others, found himself promoted above the level of his abilities. As the historian examples above reveal, Hood has often been treated unfairly. For many readers and historians alike, Hood and bloody failure at Franklin and Nashville are synonymous. He deserves a more nuanced treatment. Because of negative treatment by several well known historians, a pall of incompetence has descended over Hood's overall performance as a general officer. Objective consideration and reliance upon primary sources will enable presentation of a fair and balanced accounting.

Critical writers such as Stanley Horn, Thomas L. Connelly, Wiley Sword, and James Lee McDonough have dealt with Hood simplistically. They assert that, among other things, he was handicapped by low intelligence, psychological problems, drug use, and even the effects of a failed love affair. What all of these historians have in common, is an overemphasis upon the final six months of a military career, a career that contained so much more. At the center of their argument lies Hood's decision to launch a costly frontal assault at Franklin, Tennessee on November 30, 1864. In short, for these writers, a single event is allowed to define four years of military service to the South.

---

[33]   Sumner A. Cunningham, John A. Simpson, ed., *Reminiscences of the 41st Tennessee: The Civil War in the West,* 117. The editor states that Cunningham's narrative is based upon his well-detailed wartime diary which "testifies to the fact that he . . . recognized that he was participating in an event of truly historic proportions." Simpson comments further that the true significance of *Reminiscences* as a valuable Civil War narrative is that Cunningham's unglamorous story "reveals much about [his] human inadequacies in the face of mortal combat." For Simpson, Cunningham stands as representative of the typical Confederate soldier. (R*eminiscences,* 140)

Relatively objective biographies, such as John Dyer's *The Gallant Hood* and Richard O'Connor's *Hood: The Cavalier General,* do a good job covering the major events in the life of their subject but fail to delve deeply enough into how Southern culture and society molded the man and how well he represented his region. My work is not a biography but a study that reaches beyond Lost Cause—influenced characterizations employed by some writers on Hood. I have endeavored to provide an overview of Hood's entire military life during the Civil War. By covering every battle that he directed as commander of the Army of Tennessee, it has been possible to reveal a young general that, though overpromoted, possessed imagination and creativity in his battle plans. From his ascension to command in mid-July until the end following Nashville in December 1864, Hood ordered only one frontal assault, one dictated by the pressures of time and circumstance rather than personal whim.

I have also examined influence exerted upon Hood by his "teacher-generals," Robert E. Lee and Thomas J. Jackson, and how Southern society and culture influenced them all. Recent writers who have dealt with Hood in a more careful fashion, such as Richard McMurry, Stephen Davis, and Russell Bonds, have written mainly in the context of battles and decisions made at the time. They have not examined Hood's education as an officer or upon how Lost Cause writers constructed the myth that Hood represented an incompetent disaster for the South. This paper attempts to provide an in-depth portrait and analysis of Hood the military leader and later citizen. In order to do this, I have used primary sources such as the Official Records, letters and diaries of soldiers and officers, and contemporary writings such as Thomas Van Horne's *History of the Army of the Cumberland* and writings from the Battles and Leaders series. In all, I have worked to stay as close to original sources as possible when dealing with events of Hood's life. In analyzing the Lost Cause, a phenomenon that continues to affect historical writing, several newer works have been used such as William Blair's *Cities of the Dead: Contesting the Memory of the Civil War South, 1865-1914* (2004), Karen Cox's *Dixie's Daughters: The United Daughters of the Confederacy and Preservation of Confederate Culture* (2003), and John R. Neff's *Honoring the Civil War Dead: Commemoration and the Problems of Reconciliation* (2005). To my knowledge, the only work that covers the effect of the Lost Cause on Hood's historical memory is Brian Craig Miller's *John Bell Hood and the Fight for Civil War Memory* published in 2010, while this paper was under construction.

I argue that Hood failed in Tennessee not because of intellectual limitations but for several reasons. These include inheriting a military situation virtually doomed to failure, a Confederate command and supply structure that had disintegrated beyond repair, terrifically harsh weather conditions, poor communications, and that he faced the strongest Union army ever assembled at Atlanta. In addition, Hood came up against two of the North's best generals in Sherman and Thomas. Hood, it will be seen, though promoted beyond his experience, gave a credible effort especially in the fighting around Atlanta, displaying a bold and creative understanding of warfare.

In chapter 1, I explore how Hood learned to be a military officer. McWhiney and Jamieson, in *Attack and Die: Civil War Military Tactics and the Southern Heritage*, reveal that Confederate military and political leaders prided themselves in their bellicosity. Hood had often been accused of being overaggressive, yet the above study shows Southerners as far more likely to employ costly offensive tactics than their northern counterparts. Moreover, because of the contentious relationship existing between the regions caused by the slavery issue, secessionists as a whole possessed a touchy, "chip-on-the-shoulder" attitude toward the North. Hood and his aggressive teachers, Lee and Jackson, were far from being exceptions and well represented their region. Chapter 2 details the controversy surrounding Confederate General Joseph E. Johnston and how Hood came to inherit command of the Army of Tennessee. The four battles fought in defense of Atlanta are examined in detail, revealing Hood to be far from the stereotypical straight ahead fighter often depicted by critical historians.

The development of Confederate strategy following the fall of Atlanta and the origins for Hood's Tennessee campaign are explained in chapter 3. Here also is detailed the poor condition of the western army and its continual struggle with supply problems. A costly three-week delay at Florence, Alabama, awaiting supplies for example, virtually doomed the campaign. Also shown is Hood's attempt to isolate and destroy Union General Schofield's army of Ohio before it could join General Thomas at Nashville. The disastrous blunders at Spring Hill on September 29 are covered in great detail, culminating in the Battle of Franklin the following afternoon. Chapter 4 discusses Hood's options following Franklin and analyzes both Union and Confederate plans for the Battle of Nashville. Both Hood and Thomas had desperate need of reinforcements; Thomas received his only days before fighting began, Hood did not. Both armies struggled against a common enemy, some of the worst weather to ever strike Middle Tennessee.

Thomas's battle plans at Nashville and Hood's reaction are discussed and analyzed in chapter 5. Though the Union plan was excellent in conception and included pursuit and destruction of the Southern army, tactical and logistical problems prevented this conclusion. Nevertheless, the Army of Tennessee found itself literally driven out of the state and rendered so damaged that it would never again prove a threat in the West.

Chapter 6 explains how Civil War death on an unprecedented scale acted as a catalyst for the development of the Lost Cause. This phenomenon appeared first as an effort by Southern women to memorialize their region's war dead. It later developed into a masterful propaganda exercise whose goals were to vindicate and celebrate the Confederate cause. Lost Cause architects sought to explain away the South's loss and find scapegoats to blame. Generals John Bell Hood and

James Longstreet became its principal victims, and it is here that the origins for the Hood myth are found. The concluding chapter 7 provides an overview of the legacy of the Lost Cause and gives examples of how it continues to affect present day historiography.

CHAPTER 1

Education

John Bell Hood was born in Owingsville, Kentucky, on June 29, 1831. Two events of historical significance also occurred that year. In January, William Lloyd Garrison launched his abolitionist newspaper, the *Liberator*, in Boston and in August, witnessed the worst slave revolt in Southern history led by Nat Turner in Southampton County, Virginia.

Both parents, John W. Hood and Theodosia French, shared ancestors who played active roles during the American Revolution. As a successful country physician, Hood's father provided his family with a stable, though not wealthy, home and upbringing. In 1849, the young man received an appointment to the United States Military Academy at West Point, made possible by the recommendation of his uncle, Judge French, and then served in Congress.[34] In his memoirs, Hood recalled that "I fancied a military life, although it was not my father's choice . . . Doubtless, I . . . inherited this predilection from my grandfathers who were soldiers under Washington."[35]

At the academy, Hood shared company with many who would later distinguish themselves during the Civil War, including Phil Sheridan, J. E. B. Stuart, James McPherson, and John Schofield. Colonel Robert E. Lee became superintendent in 1852 and made a strong positive impression upon the cadets.[36]

Between 1849 and 1853, Hood's graduation year, momentous events shook the country. On March 4, 1850, South Carolina's Senator John C. Calhoun rose from his sickbed to present one of his last speeches. In it, he spoke of sinews holding the nation together and stated darkly that "agitation of the slavery question has snapped some of the most important and . . . greatly weakened all the others."[37] Calhoun

---

[34] John P. Dyer, *The Gallant Hood* (New York: Bobbs-Merrill Company, Inc., 1950), 26.

[35] Hood, *Advance and Retreat*, 5.

[36] Dyer, *The Gallant Hood*, 31.

[37] David M. Potter, *The Impending Crisis: 1848-1861* (New York: Harper and Row, 1976), 101. Taken from the speech written by Calhoun which he was too ill to deliver; though present in the chamber, Senator James M. Mason of Virginia read it for him.

argued further that once these sinews snapped, force would be required to maintain the integrity of the Union. Senator Alexander Stephens of Georgia also feared for the future of the Union. By 1852, Daniel Webster and Henry Clay, architects of the 1850 Compromise, had died. Before long, cries of "Bleeding Kansas" echoed across the land. At West Point, cadets energetically discussed public events, and their arguments often grew so heated that academy officials temporarily closed down debating societies.[38]

After graduation and upon being brevetted as a second lieutenant, Hood was sent to California. He served at San Francisco, Benicia, and Fort Jones in the northern part of the state and departed in 1855 when appointed to the newly formed 2nd Cavalry Regiment. This elite organization contained many men of future prominence: officers Albert Sydney Johnston served as colonel, Robert E. Lee as lieutenant colonel, and William Hardee and George Thomas as majors. While serving as Thomas's adjutant, Hood found the Virginian's "manliness and dignity" impressive. During his time with the cavalry, he saw Texas for the first time and developed admiration for its open spaces and beauty.[39]

In November 1860, First Lieutenant Hood received an offer to become chief of the cavalry at West Point; his mental abilities then held in higher regard than by some of today's historians. After all, men like George Thomas had held that post, and if he had not had some recognizable abilities, it would not have been offered. To the surprise of Adjutant-General Cooper, however, the young officer turned down the prestigious assignment citing as his reason the unsettled political situation in the country. Hood expressed a desire to be able to "act with entire freedom should war break out."[40]

Following the portentous events of April 1861, Hood resigned his commission in the United States Army and "repaired at the latter part of [the month] to Montgomery, Alabama," capital of the newly formed Confederacy, there to offer his services to its government.[41] From there, he journeyed to Richmond where newly promoted Major General Robert E. Lee sent him to join Colonel John Magruder at Yorktown. During this time, his series of rapid promotions began. Magruder jumped Hood over others with more seniority because he considered him more experienced than the great number of other young lieutenants commanding companies of men. By October 1861, Hood had risen to the rank of major. On July 11, he organized a highly successful ambush of Union troops using about eighty men. They netted many Yankee prisoners, the first that most Confederates had ever seen. This action caused him to rise in the estimation of his fellow soldiers. Captain Thomas F. Goode, who had taken part, remarked, "For our victory, all acknowledge

---

[38]   Dyer, *The Gallant* Hood, 33.

[39]   Hood, *Advance and Retreat*, 8.

[40]   Hood, *Advance and Retreat*, 15.

[41]   Ibid., 16.

a great indebtedness to the gallant bearing and skillful conduct of Maj. Hood, who is every inch an officer."[42] Reporting to Lee, a gleeful Magruder described the ambush as "a brilliant little affair."[43] It would not be long before he became colonel of a new regiment, the 4th Texas, and encountered his first real leadership test. According to regimental chaplain Nicholas Davis, the men who came across the plains represented "all portions of the state—young, impetuous, and fresh, full of energy, enterprise and fire—men of action."[44] The *Richmond Examiner* quipped that "such men as these will make quick work of Yankee racers when they get a chance."[45] Despite their suitability for combat, Chaplain Davis noted a serious lack of discipline at "Camp Texas."[46]

Young Colonel Hood proved equal to the task and quickly molded these independent men into a well-disciplined force. In time, as more volunteers arrived from the far reaches of the Southwest, the 4th Texas merged with the 1st and 5th Texas, 18th Georgia, and Wade Hampton's Legion of Cavalry from South Carolina to form the "Texas Brigade," which became one of the hardest-hitting units in Lee's army. In March 1862, General Lee promoted Hood to brigadier general and placed him in command. Hood's promotion over other officers holding seniority is a mystery. It could have been because he attended West Point, while others had not and that Jefferson Davis preferred professionally trained officers when he could get them. Whatever the reason, "Hood would fight his way to the attention of almost everyone concerned with . . . southern arms" and within six months of taking command acquired his sobriquet, the Gallant Hood of Texas.[47]

John Bell Hood learned his trade from Generals Lee and Jackson during nearly three and one half years of service to the Confederacy. These aggressive officers did not hesitate to take calculated risks to achieve their ends. Perhaps the most famous example is when Lee split his army in order to defeat a much larger Union force at Chancellorsville.

On May 7, 1862, the Texas Brigade conducted itself with great distinction during Union General McClellan's peninsular offensive. Confederate General D. H. Hill wrote, "A portion of the Yankee army landed at Eltham's to intercept our retreat. [Major General William B. Franklin's] whole corps had come up York River. Hood, with a single brigade, attacked their advance on the 7th and drove them back to their gunboats. Franklin troubled us no more. His experience . . . with the Texans

---

[42]   Richard M. McMurry, *John Bell Hood and the War for Southern Independence* (Lincoln: University of Nebraska, 2000), 26.

[43]   Ibid.

[44]   Donald E. Everett, ed., *Chaplain Davis and Hood's Texas Brigade* (San Antonio, 1962), 35-36, 61-62, in Richard McMurry, *John Bell Hood and the War for Southern Independence*, 28.

[45]   *Richmond Examiner*, Sept. 3, 1861, in McMurry, *John Bell Hood*, 28.

[46]   Davis Diary, September 25, 1861, in McMurry, *John Bell Hood*, 28.

[47]   McMurry, *John Bell Hood and the War for Southern Independence*, 35.

had been ample . . . . He desired no more of it."[48] Incredibly, a single rebel brigade, though greatly outnumbered, had driven back an entire Union corps.

The Battle of Gaine's Mill, June 27, 1862, provides perhaps the finest example of General Lee's orders expedited by Hood's action. Lee tried unsuccessfully for most of the day to break the Union center on Turkey Hill. The position was defended by the natural obstacle of Powite Creek and an abatis erected before the federal works, "whilst batteries supported by masses of infantry crowned the crest."[49] Hood's brigade, at that time part of General Whiting's division in Jackson's corps, arrived on the field late in the afternoon. In Jackson's absence, Lee asked Hood if the Texans could take the Union position which he regarded as "the key to the battlefield."[50] Hood replied by stating simply that he would try, and he put his brigade in motion.

The men moved forward rapidly, having been ordered not to fire until Hood gave the command; "For I knew full well that if the men were allowed to fire, they would halt to load, break the alignment, and very likely, never reach the breastworks."[51] Hood delayed until his brigade reached the creek's edge. Immediately after this, the men fixed bayonets and charged the enemy. "The onset was so furious and determined, that seized by panic, the first line of Federals . . . took to precipitate flight. Their panic communicated itself to the troops in the two lines behind them, and they, too, fled, pell-mell, and probably with a prayer that the devil might save the hindmost."[52]

The assault proved overwhelmingly successful; fourteen artillery pieces and nearly an entire New Jersey regiment fell into Confederate hands. The price, however, had been high; nearly fifty percent of the brigade fell as casualties. General Jackson wrote in his report, "The Fourth Texas, under the lead of General Hood, was the first to pierce [the enemy] strongholds and seize the guns."[53]

Historian Richard McMurry has argued that action by Hood's brigade decided the outcome, not only at Gaine's Mill, but also for the entire Seven Days campaign: "One cannot overstate the importance of the battle or of Hood's attack and the role he played in its success."[54] He notes that Lee's victory over McClellan at this time "changed the whole nature of the war. The Confederate offensive before Richmond in 1862 ended all possibility that the conflict would close quickly with relatively little

---

[48]   OR:1:XI:1, 605

[49]   Hood, *Advance and Retreat*, 26.

[50]   Hood, *Advance and* Retreat, 26.

[51]   Ibid.

[52]   J. B. Polley, *Hood's Texas Brigade*, (Dayton: Morningside, 1988), 47. Polley served in the Texas brigade, and first published this unit history in 1908 as *A Soldier's Letters to Charming Nellie*.

[53]   OR: I: IXX: II, 683.

[54]   McMurry, *John Bell Hood*, 49.

impact on the American nation."[55] One Texan remembered how Hood inspired him personally at Gaine's Mill: "I tell you what . . . I got mighty nervous and shaky while we were forming in the apple orchard to make that last desperate charge . . . But when I looked behind me and saw old Hood . . . looking as unconcerned as if he were on dress parade, I just determined that if he could stand it, I would."[56] Moreover, historian Clifford Dowdy commented that, not only had Hood shown "the instincts of [a] born fighter and a fighter's instinctive reactions," but also that "Hood's tactical initiative . . . sustained the assault of two brigades."[57]

At Antietam, Hood advanced to a divisional command consisting of two brigades: his own and that of Evander Law. On the early evening of September 17, Hood's men stepped in where others had failed. In turning back "fighting Joe" Hooker's Union corps, the Confederates paid a steep price measured in lives; out of a total of nearly two thousand men entering the action, one thousand became casualties. According to McMurry, "The first Texas lost 186 of its 226 men; the Eighteenth Georgia, 101 of its 176; and the Fourth Texas, 107 of 200." [58]

After darkness fell, Lee held a tense meeting with his generals; defeat looked inevitable. Seeking opinions about what course of action to take should McClellan choose to resume fighting the following day, he questioned his officers. An apparently overwrought Hood, when asked about readiness of his division, replied that it no longer existed. "Great God, General Hood," Lee exclaimed. "Where is the splendid division you had this morning?"[59] Hood's only answer was "they are all lying on the field where you sent them, sir, but few have straggled."[60]

McMurry comments that the summer of 1862 marked the end of Hood's military education. During this time, Hood witnessed an impressive series of Southern victories carried out against superior numbers. Most importantly, he learned that General Lee founded his tactics upon bold infantry assaults, a technique that often resulted in success though costly in human terms. Adding emphasis, J. E. B. Stuart remarked that Lee's army was "far better adapted to attack than defense."[61] Though successful during the war's first year, such tactics would later prove responsible for bleeding the Confederacy to death. One could argue that Lee's teaching doomed Hood who would later take techniques learned in Virginia to Tennessee. There he would encounter stronger Union commanders than Lee had fought in the East; Grant, Sherman, and Thomas.

---

[55] Ibid.

[56] Ibid, 49-50.

[57] Ibid.

[58] Ibid., 58-59.

[59] Dyer, *The Gallant Hood*, 143; Polley, *Hood's Texas Brigade*, 134.

[60] Ibid.

[61] Douglas Southall Freeman, *Lee's Lieutenants*, Vol. 1 (New York: Charles Scribner's Sons, 1942), 261.

Lee exerted a profound influence on Hood, and disturbing reflections of the Virginian's attacks at Malvern Hill, Antietam, and Gettysburg exist in subsequent actions by Hood at Atlanta and Franklin in 1864. For example, at Malvern Hill, Lee failed to use his artillery effectively while launching costly infantry assaults upon strong Union positions. At Franklin, Hood used the bulk of his artillery in an unsuccessful attempt to decoy Union General Schofield into expecting an attack at Columbia while using his infantry in an unsuccessful attempt to shatter a fortified Union line. Both generals employed the frontal assault in a utilitarian manner, but as we shall see, Hood had fewer options in Tennessee than did Lee in Virginia and Pennsylvania. There he would be restricted more tightly by time and would receive no reinforcements.

Hood has often been labeled by historians as overly aggressive, but Southern military and political classes prided themselves on their bellicosity. Historians Grady McWhiney and Perry Jamieson in their book, *Attack and Die: Civil War Military Tactics and the Southern Heritage*, have assembled statistical analysis that shows Southern generals as more prone to costly offensive tactics than their northern counterparts which is reflected in casualty percentages. For the entire war, Lee averaged a 20.2 percent casualty rate; Braxton Bragg, 19.5 percent; and Hood, 19.2 percent. By contrast, Union commanders show a significantly lower rate. McClellan's casualties are 9.5 percent. George Thomas, 5.0 percent; Sherman, 7.4 percent; and even Sheridan, known to be especially pugnacious, is listed at a relatively low 12.8 percent. Joe Johnston, who preferred Fabian strategy to a headlong attacking style, and Ulysses S. Grant, who stands out as the most combative of Union generals, appear as anomalies—exceptions to the rule in their respective armies. Johnston's overall casualty rate is listed at 10.5 percent and Grant's at 18.1.[62]

Confederate President Jefferson Davis's announcement in 1861 that the South would conduct an offensive-defensive war, a struggle aimed primarily at halting northern aggression, was nothing more than propaganda. McWhiney and Jamieson assert that Davis developed an appreciation for offensive tactics during his days in Mexico as Colonel of the Mississippi Rifles and that he nurtured an abiding love for mass infantry assaults. At war's beginning, Davis remarked pointedly to General Joseph Johnston that he could not allow anything to "stand in the way of the one great object, giving our columns [the] capacity to take the offensive."[63] Backing Davis up, the ever pugnacious Secretary of War, Robert Toombs, declared his support for "carrying the war into the enemy's country," only one month after hostilities began.[64] After Davis's enthusiastic speech following first Manassas in which he

---

[62]   McWhiney and Jamieson, *Attack and Die*, Table 5.

[63]   Dunbar Rowland ed., *Jefferson Davis' Constitutionalist: His Letters, Papers and Speeches*, Vol. 5 (Jackson: 1923), 338, in McWhiney and Jamieson, *Attack and Die*, 5, 6.

[64]   John B. Jones *A Rebel War Clerk's Diary*, ed. Earl S. Miers (New York: 1958), 18, 27, 36, in McWhiney and Jamieson, *Attack and Die*, 7.

declared himself ready to take the offensive, Confederate War Department Clerk John B. Jones remarked that he had "never heard . . . more hearty cheering."[65]

A series of aggressive attacks in the War's first large battles saw Confederates suffer ninety-seven thousand casualties, twenty thousand more than Union forces. These included Shiloh, the Seven Days, First Manassas, Antietam, Stones River, and Chancellorsville. Southern Generals believed in leading from the front, and as a result, "fifty-five percent . . . (235 of 425) of them were killed or wounded."[66]

John Bell Hood fit in well with this group. He suffered crippling of his left arm while organizing the attack on Devil's Den at Gettysburg, and the loss of his right leg led a breakthrough at Chickamauga. In both cases, he returned to action within a three-month period of recuperation. As the war went on, therefore, "Confederate leaders seemed to ignore the casualty lists and . . . mutilate themselves and their armies."[67]

McWhiney and Jamieson theorize that Southern aggressiveness had its origins in dominant Celtic settlement patterns. Thus, an impulsive male-dominated society attracted to violence and military themes was really an expression of ethnicity.[68] While heavily Scots-Irish emigration to the Carolinas and Western Virginia and domination of Virginia's Chesapeake by Cavalier elites are well documented, stronger forces worked in developing perception among Southerners of cultural isolation and a unique sense of identity. Over time, such feelings strengthened, and a defensive-aggressive outlook emerged, in effect a siege mentality which reflected the corrosive effects of the region's reliance upon African slavery.

Southern dependence upon cash crop agriculture and slave labor began with tobacco in Virginia and expanded to rice and sugar in what was called "Carolina" during the 1600s. By contrast, the isolating influence of England's Civil Wars caused New England to diversify and become self-reliant. Historians John McCusker and Russell Menard comment that "the Yankee merchant, born of necessity, quickly became the masters of the New World's commerce."[69] Aggressive commercialism, combined with Puritan moral values, irritated Southern aristocrats like Sir William Berkeley, Virginia's governor from 1641 to 1677 who drove New Englanders out of Virginia and expressed disdain for their social values: "I thank God there are no free schools nor printing [in Virginia] and hope we shall not have these [for a] hundred

---

65 McWhiney and Jamieson, *Attack and Die,* 7.

66 Ibid., 14.

67 McWhiney and Jamieson, *Attack and* Die, 15.

68 Ibid., 172.

69 John J. McCusker and Russell R. Menard, *The Economy of British America, 1607-1789* (Chapel Hill: University of North Carolina Press, 1985), 101.

years; for learning has brought disobedience and heresy . . . into the world."[70] For Berkeley, keeping the lower classes poor and ignorant helped maintain proper order in society. Such thinking persisted among Southern classes into the 1860s and beyond.

Bacon's Rebellion in 1676 acted as a catalyst for Virginia's aristocrats, forcing the realization that they could no longer rely upon or subjugate white farmers. From this point onward, planters developed a rapidly increasing dependence upon African slave labor. Using legal codes inherited from Barbados, they made the Peculiar Institution an integral part of Southern culture and society. On the eve of the Revolution, New England, particularly Massachusetts, stood at the forefront in resistance to crown control. Though the Southern colonies agreed to support their northern brethren, a feeling of difference had begun to assert itself. While organizing the Continental Army in the wake of events at Lexington and Concord in 1775, Virginian George Washington expressed his poor opinion of New England soldiers, referring to them as "an exceedingly dirty and nasty people."[71] Moreover, he felt offended by what he called their "leveling spirit" and "was unprepared for the [commercialism of] New England where every farmer fancied himself a merchant."[72] That Washington later softened his harsh opinions does not change the fact that a distinct feeling of regional difference existed and grew stronger with the passage of time.

Following war's end in 1783, the South compacted itself, further increasing its dependence upon big agriculture and chattel slavery. The North, on the other hand, continued to diversify. Acquisition of vast new territories resulting from the Louisiana Purchase and the War with Mexico accelerated competition between the sections for land and political power.

Regional aggravation reached a crescendo in the 1850s, following the last compromise that over California's admission as a free state. Key events of this crucial decade read like the tolling of a funeral bell: the Kansas-Nebraska Act of 1854, the beating of Massachusetts Senator Charles Sumner by Senator Preston Brooks of South Carolina in 1856, the Dred Scott decision in 1857, and John Brown's Raid on Harper's Ferry in 1859. By 1860, the two sections stood like fighters ready to square off in the ring. Indeed, Senator John Sherman of Ohio stated the case bluntly, "There is really no Union now between the North and South . . . . No two nations

---

[70]   Alan Taylor, *American Colonies: The Settling of North America* (New York: Penguin Books, 2001), 147. For further commentary on 19th century southern educational opportunities see Sean Wilentz, *The Rise of American Democracy: Jefferson to Lincoln* (New York: W. W. Norton, 2005), 732, 733.

[71]   Philander Chase et al., eds., *The Papers of George Washington: Revolutionary War Series* (Charlottesville, 1985), 335, 372, in Jack Rakove, *Revolutionaries: A New History of the Invention of America* (New York: Houghton Mifflin Harcourt, 2010), 122.

[72]   Rakove, *Revolutionaries*, 122.

upon earth entertain feelings of more bitter rancor toward each other than these two sections of the Republic."[73] During these years, young Southerners like John Bell Hood became concerned that Northerners intended to subjugate the South by threatening its economic system or, as they put it, their "way of life."

Historian Gary Gallagher aptly contrasts two views entertained by scholars: first, that by Lincoln's election the North and South had developed into contrasting civilizations; and second, that commonalities such as shared history and language outweighed actual differences. Gallagher emphasizes, however, that the crucial point really lies in how much "Northerners and Southerners *believed* they were different."[74] Southerners labeled all Northerners as grasping "Yankees," while Northerners saw their counterparts as cruel and arrogant slave drivers, especially after publication of Harriet Beecher Stowe's *Uncle Tom's Cabin* in 1852.

In 1860, John Bell Hood elected to resign from the United States Army and seek service with the South. Richard O'Connor commented that Hood "considered himself a southerner by birth and sympathy. Unlike many United States army officers who joined the Confederacy, he [suffered no qualms] over the righteousness of placing his loyalty to the South above . . . duty to the Federal government."[75] In short, Hood identified with his region, including its culture, politics, and economic structure and felt bound to defend it.

Following Antietam, General Jackson recommended Hood for promotion to major general. His communication to the Confederate War Department reads, "It gives me great pleasure to say that [Hood's] duties were discharged with such ability and zeal as to command my admiration. I regard him as one of the most promising officers of the army."[76] Lee endorsed Jackson's recommendation in a letter to Secretary of War, George W. Randolph, dated October 27, 1862: "Brigadier General J. B. Hood is recommended to be promoted to major general to command Hood's division."[77] Hood gained the admiration of his superior officers because he carried out their aggressive tactics so well and could be trusted to follow orders.

Gettysburg marked the only time Hood disagreed with Lee's plans. In voicing dissent, he joined Lieutenant General James Longstreet. Instead of assaulting Union troops securely ensconced behind rocks and timber breastworks on the high

---

[73]   Benson Bobrick, *General George H. Thomas & the Most Decisive Battle of the Civil War: The Battle of Nashville* (New York: Alfred Knopf, 2010), 17, 18.

[74]   Gary W. Gallagher, *The American Civil War: Great Courses in Modern History* lecture series, Part 1. (Chantilly, Va., The Teaching Company, 2000).

[75]   Richard O'Connor, *Hood, Cavalier General* (New York: Prentice Hall Inc., 1949), 18.

[76]   Hood, *Advance and Retreat, 45.* Biographer John Dyer noted that the original letter to General Samuel Cooper, dated September 27, 1862, was undoubtedly included with Hood's papers when he died in New Orleans. Their fate is a mystery, but it is thought that they were carelessly burned as trash. See Dyer, *The Gallant Hood*, Note 54, p. 341.

[77]   OR: 1:19:2:683.

ground in Devils Den, Hood favored a bold flanking movement, reminiscent of those carried out by Stonewall Jackson at Second Manassas and Chancellorsville. Lee remained adamant, however, and the attack failed with heavy casualties. Hood suffered a crippling wound to his left arm from exploding shell fragments while organizing his men for attack. A few days after the battle, British observer Colonel Arthur Fremantle saw General Hood riding in a carriage and remarked that "he looked rather bad and has been suffering a great deal; the doctors seem to doubt whether they will be able to save his arm."[78]

It can be argued that Hood's early exit had a significant effect upon Lee's attack plan which involved moving up the Emmitsburg Road to roll up the Union left flank. Historian Stephen Sears writes that at Gettysburg, "Hood was perhaps the most highly regarded fighting general in the Army of Northern Virginia," a man who preferred to lead "by inspiration and from up front."[79] His division had the task of spearheading the Confederate effort. The beginning of the attack saw fierce Union resistance and broken ground combine to divert Hood's regiments from their appointed paths. Sears remarks that at this critical moment, Hood stood ready to "untangle [things] . . . or at least manage" the assault but received a wound that removed him from the field." Getting General Evander Law to take over not only caused delay, but he proved a less dynamic influence. Thus, Lee's attack ran out of steam.[80]

Three months later, driven by duty and combative spirit, Hood rejoined his division in Georgia as part of Longstreet's Corps to reinforce Braxton Bragg's Army of Tennessee at Chickamauga. On September 20, 1863, the second day of the war's bloodiest battle in the West, Hood led his men forward in what proved to be the key breakthrough of the Union line. During the assault, a mini ball shattered his left thigh just below the hip. As he fell from his horse, men from the Texas Brigade caught him. Amid the carnage of Chickamauga and in the wake of Confederate victory, rumors of Hood's death circulated quickly. General Lee in Virginia wrote to Jefferson Davis, "I am grieved to learn of the death of General Hood" and further stated, "I am gradually losing my best men—Jackson, Pender, Hood!"[81] Four days later, however, Lee was able to write the president again, this time expressing his "great relief" that Hood had survived.[82] The injury, though grave, proved only a temporary impediment to Hood's military career.

---

[78]   Lieutenant Colonel Arthur J. L. Fremantle, *Three Months in the Southern States-April-June 1863* (Lincoln: University of Nebraska Press, 1991), 282.

[79]   Stephen W. Sears, *Gettysburg* (New York: Houghton Mifflin Company, 2003), 265.

[80]   Sears, *Gettysburg*, 68.

[81]   Clifford Dowdey and Louis H. Manarin eds., *The Wartime Papers of R. E. Lee* (New York: Bramhall House, 1946), 603. Lee to Davis, September 23, 1863

[82]   Ibid., September 27, 1863.

John Bell Hood learned his leadership skills in a school that taught belligerent offensive tactics. Lee rarely used defensive techniques, and his aristocratic demeanor belied cold-blooded aggressiveness on the battlefield. When students admire and respect teachers, it is only natural that they should attempt emulation. Though his connections to Lee stretched back to West Point and the 2nd Cavalry, it seems that General T. J Jackson, the mighty Stonewall, master of the flank attack, most influenced Hood. One practice he may have inherited from observing General Lee was that of issuing discretionary orders to subordinates. Up until the debacle of Pickett's Charge at Gettysburg, the Virginian leaned toward verbal rather than written orders, a practice which allowed his officers latitude in interpretation. For Hood, the events at Spring Hill on November 29, 1864, demonstrate this policy played out to disastrous effect.[83]

Hood paid a high personal price for being such a good student as did the men he led into battle. This included severe physical and psychological injury as well as death. Though no definitive evidence exists to support the idea, such trauma bears consideration when viewing his subsequent performance. In better times, a soldier in his condition would have been retired from duty, but the growing and severe shortage of experienced officers in the Confederacy precluded such policy.

---

[83]   Stephen W. Sears, *Gettysburg*, 504; McMurry, *John Bell Hood*, 129.

CHAPTER 2

Into the Vortex

General John Bell Hood first experienced action with the Army of Tennessee at Chickamauga on September 19 and 20, 1863. In leading the crucial breakthrough of the Union center spearheaded by Longstreet's corps, Hood lost his right leg and tasted the mixture of glory and misfortune often associated with the Confederacy's western army. Seemingly, its ill-starred career began in Shiloh when its first commander, Albert Sidney Johnston, bled to death while his soldiers pushed Grant's army to the wall on the battle's first day. From that point, its fortunes followed a descending path.

Jefferson Davis asked Hood to join the Army of Tennessee and its commander, General Joseph E. Johnston, after he recovered from his injury. Hood agreed and looked forward to an aggressive campaign against Sherman in Georgia. Unfortunately, Johnston disappointed the Confederate president and Congress by conducting a series of strategic withdrawals from May to mid-July 1864. Along with his failure to fight a decisive battle, Johnston gave up one hundred miles of territory and lost over twenty thousand soldiers to death, injury, and desertion. He was replaced by Hood on July 17. After much deliberation, Davis chose Hood because of his proven record as a fighting general. In response, the Kentuckian fought four battles in forty-six days, attempting to break the ever-tightening Union noose around Atlanta. His battle plans at Peachtree Creek on July 20, the Battle of Atlanta on July 22, and Ezra Church on July 28 reveal Hood to have been far more than the straight-ahead fighter too often depicted by historians.

Following Chickamauga, Hood recovered health rapidly, stating that "by the middle of January 1864, I was again able to mount my horse and enjoy exercise."[84] During his convalescent period in the Confederate capital, Hood frequently associated with Jefferson Davis, often taking part in the president's morning rides. He remarked upon being "afforded . . . [the] opportunity to become well acquainted with this extraordinary man and illustrious patriot of the South."[85] When asked to join

---

[84] Hood, *Advance and Retreat,* 67.

[85] Ibid.

General Joseph E. Johnston's army then in winter quarters at Dalton, Georgia, Hood "cheerfully acquiesced . . . but with the understanding that an aggressive campaign would be initiated."[86] As noted in chapter 1, Davis favored an offensive-defensive strategy. That is, he expected commanders not only to defend Southern territory, but to be active and operate with the view of attacking and destroying Union armies whenever possible. Indeed, the president had told Johnston in 1861 that nothing should interfere with the overall object of taking the offensive.[87] In short, neither Davis nor anyone else knew how Johnston would behave during the upcoming Atlanta campaign. At this point, the Army of Tennessee numbered at approximately seventy thousand effectives and still possessed great potential.[88] It was not the decimated force that Hood would inherit later that summer.

Promoted to the rank of lieutenant general and serving as a corps commander, Hood, along with Davis and others, watched with dismay as Johnston consistently employed a Fabian strategy of strategic withdrawal across Georgia. Johnston preferred to select positions of great natural strength, entrenched, and then invited Sherman to attack. He did little or nothing to actively discourage Union maneuvers to flank him out of position and obdurately refused to employ his cavalry to attack Sherman's long and vulnerable supply line. Instead, he insisted that Davis order General Nathan Bedford Forrest then defending Mississippi to take on the task. Historian Richard McMurry comments that "it is about as certain as any hypothetical thing can be that an effort to use Forrest against the [western and Atlantic railroad] in northern Georgia would, at the most, have resulted in only slight damage to the railroad and might well have led to the capture and dispersal of Forrest's raiding force."[89] He remarks further that the mere *threat* of Forrest getting involved may have caused Sherman to "divert scores of units that otherwise would have joined the Yankee armies in Johnston's front."[90] For these reasons, and the fact that Davis felt Johnston's own cavalry under Joe Wheeler sufficient for the task, the president

---

[86]   Ibid.

[87]   Chapter 1, 17.

[88]   Hood, *Advance and Retreat*, 71-76; OR: I: XLVII, 1311. The *Official Records* reference comes from Jefferson Davis's report, submitted in February, 1865. In it he argued that Johnston possessed eighty-five thousand effectives at Dalton, but this figure is controversial and open to debate. In his "Reply to General Johnston," in *Advance and Retreat*, Hood took great pains to arrive at an accurate number and conservatively estimated the army at seventy thousand effectives.

[89]   Richard McMurry, *Atlanta 1864: Last Chance for the Confederacy* (Lincoln: University of Nebraska, 2000), 200-201; Steven Davis, "A Reappraisal of the Generalship of John Bell Hood in the Battle of Atlanta," in *The Campaign for Atlanta and Sherman's March to the Sea: Essays of the 1864 Campaigns,* Volume I, eds., Theodore P. Savas and David A. Woodbury (Campbell, CA: Savas Woodbury Publishers, 1992), 52.

[90]   Ibid.

refused to consider moving Forrest. Moreover, the South could no more afford to lose Mississippi than Georgia. We can speculate that had Johnston made a definitive effort to disturb Sherman's lifeline, the Union commander would have been forced to pull more troops away from his front to defend it. This would have resulted, at least, in delaying his advance. Hypothetical aside, what we do know is that Johnston made no such efforts and continued to pull back. After failing to defend strong positions at Kennesaw Mountain, and his strongest yet, in front of the Chattahoochee River, Davis finally lost patience with his general. Historian Albert Castel writes that Davis was helped to his decision by "statements from those in a position to know, among them Hardee—all to the effect that Johnston has had a number of opportunities to attack to advantage but that every time he has refused to avail himself of them." For the president, "the contrast to Lee is damning. Right from the start, Lee pounced on Grant, and even now, while defending a twenty-six-mile line with fewer than forty thousand men, he lashes out fiercely whenever the enemy tries to outflank him."[91]

The Confederate president wired Johnston on July 16, stating directly, "I wish to hear from you as to [your] present situation and your plan of operations *so specifically* as will enable me to anticipate events."[92] Davis clearly asked for specifics, and Johnston well knew that many had become disenchanted with his conduct of the war in Georgia, yet he replied like a truculent schoolboy, "As the enemy has double my number, we must be on the defensive. My plan of operations must, therefore, depend upon that of the enemy."[93] In other words, Johnston had no plan of his own; instead, he allowed Sherman to dictate what his next move would be. Historian Stephen Davis writes that "by these retreats, it seems that the only way Joe Johnston foiled Sherman's plans . . . was by evacuation before . . . Yankee plans could take effect."[94] Johnston's own chief of staff, Brigadier General William W. MacKall, underlined the doleful Confederate situation, "Nothing brilliant has been done; nothing of the kind may be done."[95]

Could Joe Johnston or Hood have kept Sherman out of Atlanta until after the 1864 election? By mid-July, Sherman's army had crossed the Chattahoochee and assembled itself outside the city of Atlanta. For John Bell Hood to have held out until either slightly before or after November 8, the day of presidential voting, would have required either a great mistake on Sherman's part or some form of divine intervention. As shall be discussed, Hood and his army put forth a credible struggle and held the unionists at bay for forty-five days. By the time Hood took

---

[91] Albert Castel, *Decision in the West: The Atlanta Campaign of 1864* (Lawrence: University Press of Kansas, 1992), 345.

[92] OR: I: XXXVIII: V, 882.

[93] Ibid., 883.

[94] Stephen Davis, "A Reappraisal," in Savas and Woodbury, 50.

[95] Stephen Davis, "A Reappraisal," in Savas and Woodbury, 51.

command, the Tennessee Army had been reduced by over twenty thousand.[96] Hood fought three battles in eight days in efforts not only to defend the city but also to defeat Sherman in detail. A final battle fought at Jonesboro on September 1 and 2, contended for the last rail link with the Confederacy. Once that was lost, Hood had no choice but to withdraw. Though some historians have criticized these battles as fruitless, "Hood deserves much more credit for his battle plans and deserves less personal blame for the failure of his subordinates to carry them out."[97]

Johnston had the best chance of delaying Atlanta's fall until after Election Day. In order to do this, however, he would have had to have actively defended all of his fortified positions beginning at Dalton in May. Elements of his army would have had to sally forth from behind their defensive lines and then attacked Union troops attempting to flank them out of position. Johnston could have done this from virtually every position where he took a stand instead of passively sitting behind his entrenchments hoping that Sherman would make the mistake of launching a frontal assault. Davis writes that "Johnston's fearfulness and lack of aggression were particularly evident as the Confederate army neared the Chattahoochee River—the last major geographical barrier between Sherman and Atlanta." In evaluating Johnston, historian Robert K. Krick comments that his personality reflected "prudence to or perhaps beyond the threshold of timorousness."[98] How long could Johnston have delayed Sherman? How much could he have damaged the Union army? We can never know the answers to these questions because Johnston never tried; when backed up against the Chattahoochee, for example, "he never sought an opportunity to strike the enemy."[99] Much is made of the fact that Hood experienced greater casualties in a week than Johnston had in three months, but Hood fought on the offensive, which is always more costly, and did not give up one hundred miles of territory while doing so.[100]

By July 17, 1864, General Joseph Johnston had completely lost the confidence of Jefferson Davis. Not long after sending his noncommittal reply to the president's request for specific details of his plans, Johnston received a curt message from Adjutant-General Samuel Cooper which read:

---

[96]   OR: I: XLV: XLVII, 1311; Hood, *Advance and Retreat*, 72. Hood revealed that Johnston lost over eight thousand men to desertion during the last twenty miles of his retreat to Atlanta and commented that desertion was worse in its effect than death as "the deserter generally takes with him his arms and demoralizes the comrades he has forsaken."

[97]   Davis, "A Reappraisal," in Savas and Woodbury, 61.

[98]   Robert k. Krick, "Snarl and Sneer and Quarrel," in *Leaders of the Lost Cause: New Perspectives on the Confederate High Command*, eds., Gary Gallagher and Joseph T. Glatthar (Mechanicsburg, PA: Stackpole Books, 2004), 165.

[99]   Stephen Davis, "A Reappraisal," in Savas and Woodbury, 50.

[100] Ibid., 50-51.

> Lieutenant General J. B. Hood has been commissioned to the temporary
> rank of general under the late law of Congress. I am directed by the
> Secretary of War to inform you that as you have failed to arrest the advance
> of the enemy to the vicinity of Atlanta, far in the interior of Georgia, *and
> express no confidence that you can defeat of repel him,* you are hereby relieved
> from the command of the Army and Department of Tennessee which you
> will immediately turn over to General Hood.[101]

Hood received a message from the Secretary of War which read in part, "You are charged with a great trust. You will, I know, test to the utmost your capacities to discharge it."[102] Hood thus took command under some of the most difficult circumstances encountered by any general in history. It would indeed prove a "test to the utmost."

Removing a general from command in the midst of a campaign represented a very difficult decision for Davis. He agonized over it for seven days before finally arriving at his decision. His choice of Hood over Johnston aroused indignation in some quarters, particularly among officers loyal to the Virginian. A view of Hood as a relative newcomer to the Tennessee army, and that he held junior status to General Hardee, may well have exacerbated the problem. Hardee made his objection plain by tendering his resignation to Davis, which the president denied. Without Hardee, Hood would have had no experienced commanders at corps level. Alexander Stewart, for example, had never commanded anything larger than a division before.

Formidable problems at the general officer level surfaced immediately in Hood's old corps. While Carter Stevenson should have been next in line, neither Hood nor the Confederate high command felt good about placing such an inexperienced officer in this post. Instead, they chose Stephen Dill Lee then in Mississippi. Hood chose Divisional Commander Benjamin Franklin Cheatham to act in the interim. Cheatham, a Johnston loyalist known to be a hard fighter and popular with the troops, had problems of his own. Several officers claimed that he had "on various occasions been drunk on duty." At bottom, Cheatham's selection rested upon his troop leadership skills and the stipulation that the appointment would be temporary.[103]

Hood faced not only disadvantages militarily but also considerable organizational and political problems within his command structure. McMurry comments that he had "to defend Atlanta with one infantry corps commander (Hardee) who clearly resented the new . . . [situation] . . . , another (Cheatham) who may have, three (Cheatham, Stewart, and Lee) who were new to the responsibilities of corps

---

[101]   OR: I: XXVIII: V, 885.

[102]   Ibid.

[103]   McMurry, *Atlanta 1864,* 143; Davis, "A Reappraisal," in Savas and Woodbury, 52-53.

command, and one (Cheatham) who had given serious cause to doubt his fitness for a high position."[104]

It has been asserted that Hood deliberately undermined Johnston by expressing frustration with that general's lack of aggressiveness. On balance, however, others within the army did the same. Stewart posed a question to Davis's military adviser, Braxton Bragg, in March: "Are we to hold still, remaining on the defensive . . . until [Sherman] comes down to drive us out?"[105] Hardee himself complained to the president on June 22 that "if the present situation continues, we may find ourselves in Atlanta before a serious battle is fought."[106] Many of these voices came from Johnston loyalists. Bishop-General Leonidas Polk's "aide and son-in-law remarked [for example] that "General J. is not the man we thought him" and moreover "that Johnston had failed "beyond doubt, and I fear beyond repair."[107]

Historian Thomas Connelly reveals that others, better situated than Hood, worked for Johnston's removal. Braxton Bragg, who commanded the Tennessee army longer than anyone else and served as Chief of Confederate Armies, topped the list. On July 15, with Union troops threatening to cross the Chattahoochee, Bragg summed up the opinions of some of the army's generals:

> General Hood has been in favor of giving battle and mentioned to me numerous instances of opportunities lost . . . . General Hardee generally favored the retiring policy though frequently noncommittal. Lieutenant General Stewart . . . has firmly and uniformly sustained the aggressive policy. The commanding general . . . has ever been opposed to seeking battle though willing to receive it on his own terms in his chosen position.[108]

Connelly notes that Bragg's influence has often been underestimated by historians but that he held considerable sway both with the president and in military circles. Others included Secretary of War, James Seddon; Georgia senator, Benjamin Hill; and secretary of state, Judah P. Benjamin, who had formed an opinion of Johnston after he had nearly given up Richmond in 1861: "From a close observation of his career, I became persuaded that his nervous dread of losing a battle would prevent at all times his ability to cope with an enemy of nearly equal strength." Seddon stated that in his opinion, Johnston "did not intend to fight a battle for

---

[104]   Ibid.

[105]   Bragg MSS in McMurry, *John Bell Hood*, 98.

[106]   Davis Papers, Hardee to Davis, June 22, 1864, in Thomas Connelly, *Autumn of Glory* (Baton Rouge: LSU Press, 1971), 407.

[107]   Gale Diary, May 21, 1864, in Connelly, *Autumn of Glory*, 366.

[108]   OR: I: XXXIX: II, 713.

the relief of Atlanta but was already arranging, by another disastrous retreat, to abandon his position there and elude the threatening enemy."[109]

Opposition to Johnston's removal, however, emerged among some of the troops. Captain Samuel Foster of the 12th Texas cavalry remarked that "for the first time, we hear men openly talk about going home . . . at all hours of the afternoon can be heard hurrahs for Joe Johnson [sic] and God D__ n Jeff. Davis."[110] Nurse Fannie Beers, remembering the atmosphere in crowded hospitals, wrote, "Convalescents walked about with lagging steps and gloomy faces. In every ward, men wept bitterly and groaned aloud."[111] Perhaps much of this frustration aimed more at Johnston's lack of success and constant retreat, the presence of a superior Union army, and war weariness. Recent historical writings have come to recognize the demoralizing effects of Johnston's "retrogressive policy upon the morale of the Army of Tennessee."[112] McMurry writes that "what seems to have happened was that many of Johnston's men who began the campaign with high hope gradually lost confidence as the army fell back, and then doubt began to creep into their minds about the safety of Atlanta, the Confederacy's prospects for victory, and the ability of their commander to defeat Sherman."[113] More recently, historian Larry Daniel remarked, after researching the letters and diaries of Confederate soldiers in the West, that "those who claim that Johnston's retreats did not adversely affect morale do so in the face of significant evidence to the contrary."[114] McMurry notes that the myth of Johnston's popularity largely stems from postwar writings of former soldiers able to view the entire campaign through the prism of "Hood's failure and southern defeat as a whole."[115]

Though civilians did not share the experiences and privations of soldiers, their feelings about Johnston's removal are nonetheless interesting. Newspapers across the South covered this important event, and on July 19, 1864, the *Richmond Whig* printed these comments: "Of General Johnston's merits, the country is well

---

[109]   Dunbar Rowland, ed., *Jefferson Davis Constitutionalist: His Letters, Papers, and Speeches* (Jackson, 1923), Volume 7, 320; Ibid; 8, 78, 349-354, 356; Davis, "A Reappraisal," in Savas and Woodbury, 53.

[110]   Norman Brown, ed., *One of Cleburne's Command: The Civil War Reminiscences and Diary of Captain Samuel T. Foster, Greenburg's Texas Brigade, CSA* (Austin: University of Texas Press, 1980), 106-107.

[111]   Fannie Beers, *Memories: A Record of Personal Experience and Adventure during the Years of War* (Philadelphia, 1889), 138.

[112]   Davis, "A Reappraisal," in Savas and Woodbury, 49.

[113]   Richard M. McMurry, "Confederate Morale in the Atlanta Campaign of 1864," *Georgia Historical Quarterly*, 54 (1970), 233.

[114]   Larry Daniel, *Soldiering in the Army of Tennessee: A Portrait of Life in the Confederate Army* (Chapel Hill: 1991) 141-142, in Davis, "A Reappraisal," Savas and Woodbury, 49.

[115]   McMurry, "Confederate Morale," 233.

aware, but his habit of retreating has been so often indulged in that it has long since became weary of it to a point bordering on nausea."[116] Social gatherings provided another chance to discuss events in the West. Sally "Buck" Preston, rumored to be Hood's fiancé, responded to questions about friends in the Army of Tennessee by answering, "We have not seen them in months" and noted, "They are backing down into the Gulf of Mexico with Joe Johnston."[117]

A strategy of luring Union forces into the vastness of the South and gradually draining them of their strength, as the Russians employed with Napoleon, might well have worked if carried out with government and military unanimity in 1861. Indeed, historian Gary Gallagher is of the opinion that the South's vast territory represented a valuable strategic resource. By 1864, however, the majority of military commanders, civil authority, and civilian populations had committed themselves to a policy of aggression.

In 1861, Jefferson Davis expressed caution couched in combative language. Northern invaders, he declared, would "smell Southern powder and feel Southern steel."[118] In this, he implied a defensive policy, aggressive only toward northern incursions. By 1864, the president's inherent pugnaciousness, combined with public pressure and the South's increasingly perilous position, produced demands for definitive aggressive action from its generals. In giving in to his own nature and public pressure, Davis became the victim of paradox—the more he attempted to satisfy Confederate citizens, the more unpopular he became. Historian Paul Escott comments that soldiers and citizens alike blamed him for lack of military success and even accused him of becoming a dictator. In May, the *Charleston Mercury* commented that Davis headed a government intent upon establishing "despotic authority"; and in December, *the Richmond Examiner* complained that "every military misfortune of this country is . . . due to the personal interference of Mr. Davis."[119] Davis's personality added to his woes. Escott describes him as "a high strung man who tended to be snappish"; and Confederate Secretary of War, James Seddon, called his president "the most difficult man to get along with that he had ever seen."[120]

Unlike Abraham Lincoln, who welcomed political adversaries into his cabinet in recognition of their individual talents, Davis allowed personal prejudices to drive his decisions. Diarist Mary Chesnut noted that "the president detests Joe

---

[116]   Dyer, *The Gallant Hood*, 251.

[117]   Chesnut, *A Diary from Dixie*, 419.

[118]   Sean Wilentz, *The Rise of American Democracy-Jefferson to Lincoln* (New York: W. W. Norton & Company, 2005), 777. Note 22, 947: "Arrival of President Davis in Montgomery-His Speech," in Rowland, *Davis*, 5: 48.

[119]   Paul D. Escott, *After Secession: Jefferson Davis and the Failure of Confederate Nationalism* (Baton Rouge: Louisiana State University Press, 1978), 259.

[120]   Ibid., 261-262. Note 9: *Varina Howell Davis, A Memoir*, II, 163.

Johnston . . . and General Joe returns the compliment with compound interest."[121] Johnston's removal concentrated both public and military objections to the way their government prosecuted the war. In placing Hood in command, Davis tied him to dissatisfaction, and animosity directed toward himself. For many, Hood became a scapegoat for Confederate military failure, a taint that has influenced his treatment by historians ever since.

Besides Hood, Davis had three other choices to replace the popular Johnston; the most senior being William Hardee, followed by Lieutenant General Stephen Dill Lee, and Major General Patrick Cleburne. When the president sought Robert E. Lee's opinion, he received a rather noncommittal response: "Hood is a good fighter, very industrious on the battlefield, careless off. I have had no opportunity of judging his action when the whole responsibility rested upon him. I have a high opinion of his gallantry, earnestness, and zeal. General Hardee has more experience in managing an army."[122]

Three factors may have influenced Davis against Hardee; he was personally antagonistic toward Braxton Bragg, the president's top military advisor, he had turned down command offered in 1863, and finally, a feeling existed that he would only continue Johnston's policies. S. D. Lee, younger than Hood, lacked the Kentuckian's impressive combat resume. Cleburne, though possessing an impeccable combat record, had become the victim of politics. Being foreign born presented one problem, but the fact that he had supported use of black troops in exchange for their freedom after the war, essentially doomed any prospect of his rising beyond command of a division.[123]

Thus, Davis chose Hood. The president sought an aggressive general, and public opinion demanded something more positive and active in the West. Johnston's policy had been interpreted as essentially negative, for it had moved the army ever further South, leaving conquered territory in its wake. Hood's appointment to full generalship, however, alarmed some of his friends and supporters; many feared for the integrity of his reputation. In a conversation with Mary Chestnut, Texas Senator Louis Wigfall exclaimed, "Go at once and get Hood to decline to take the command. It will destroy him if he accepts it! He will have to fight under Jeff Davis' orders. That no one can do now and not lose caste in the western army."[124] Wigfall's comments indicate the poisonous effects a close association with Jeff Davis could bring. Other sources expressed optimism. On July 19, the *Richmond Enquirer* announced, "We are

[121]   Chesnut, *A Diary from Dixie*, 317.

[122]   Dowdy and Manarin, eds., *The Wartime Papers of Robert E. Lee*, 82.

[123]   Bruce Levine, *Confederate Emancipation-Southern Plans to Free and Arm the Slaves during the Civil War* (New York: Oxford, 2006), 2-3.

[124]   Chesnut, *A Diary from Dixie*, 419.

[now] ready to fight instead of retreat . . . the appointment has but one meaning and that is to give battle to the foe."[125]

Sherman reacted with satisfaction to the news that Johnston had been replaced. He believed that at last the rebels would emerge from their entrenchments and fight the open field battle that he had so long desired. When he asked General Schofield, who had known Hood at West Point, what the new Confederate commander was like, he received confirmation for his thoughts. Schofield answered, "I will tell you what sort of man he is. He'll hit you like hell now before you know it." General Oliver Otis Howard agreed and described Hood as "a hard fighter [who] does very unexpected things."[126] Sherman expected Hood to aim first at General James Birdseye McPherson and the Army of the Tennessee, at that point approaching Atlanta from the East and moving in isolation from Sherman's other army groups. Fulfilling Howard's prophecy, however, Hood had other plans.

Confederate scouts revealed that Sherman had made a critical tactical error. In advancing his combined armies toward the city, he left gaps between the different commands, most significantly that between Schofield and Thomas who moved North of the city. Hood planned to hit Thomas before he could affect a crossing of Peach Tree Creek, a "difficult stream . . . difficult not only for its unpredictable depth, breadth, and current, each of which varied . . . depending on recent rainfall but also for its steep banks and rocky bottom."[127] Hood hoped to catch Thomas's army in an angle formed by the confluence of the Chattahoochee and the creek. He planned an *en echelon* attack where each element would go forward like dominoes falling, one after the other, using the divisions of two of his three corps, those of Hardee and Stewart. In theory, Hood planned for the assault to begin with a strike by Bate's division on the exposed Union left to be followed in quick succession by blows from the divisions of Walker, Maney, Loring, Walthall, and French. The attack would thunder from the Confederate right to its left, crushing unsuspecting Unionists either in the act of crossing the creek or who as yet had not had time to entrench.

Two factors, one natural and the other manmade, combined to cause Southern plans to go awry. Hood decided to go forward, screened by uneven and heavily wooded terrain in the early morning hours, and to launch his assault at 1:00 p.m. Scouts revealed, however, that McPherson, marching rapidly to the East had an opportunity to outflank Cheatham's corps, placed to the far right of Hood's force. To counter this unforeseen emergency, the entire army, from French's division of Stewart's corps, stationed on the southern left to Cheatham nearly three miles away, would have to side step to the right far enough to counter McPherson. This

---

[125]   Dyer, *The Gallant Hood*, 251.

[126]   Russell S. Bonds, *War Like the Thunderbolt: The Battle and Burning of Atlanta* (Yardley, PA: Westholme Publishing LLC, 2009), 80.

[127]   Ibid., 88.

contingency, when combined with rough and uneven terrain, caused Hood's textbook-perfect plan to unravel. Cheatham moved too far which caused Hardee to hesitate. He wondered whether he should attack on time, or keep moving sideward in order to maintain contact with Cheatham. General Bate, whose division was supposed to flank the "in-the-air" Union far left, also moved too far. When the attack finally went forward at around 3:30 p.m., his troops charged "blind through the heavy woods, not only into the yawning gap between Thomas and Schofield but also into the deep valley of Clear Creek."[128] Effectively, Bate's division had removed itself from battle. The next division in Hardee's corps, that of General H. T. Walker, though greatly hampered by the vine-entangled ground, nevertheless broke through to threaten Union General Newton, positioned on the Federal far left. Before long, Yankee soldiers heard "the bloodcurdling wail of the rebel yell" even in the midst of artillery and musket fire.[129] A sergeant remembered seeing General Thomas whose headquarters lay behind Newton's lines, seated on a pile of fence rails, intently watching the battle's progress through field glasses. Thomas directed his attention toward the tree line from which Confederate General Walker's troops would soon appear. At that moment, a courier rode up in great haste and announced that "Major McGraw presents his compliments and says to inform you that the enemy is moving on him en masse, and it will be impossible to hold his position." The unflappable Thomas replied calmly, "Orderly, return to Major McGraw, give him my compliments, and tell him to hold his position. I will attend to those fellows as soon as they get out from behind the woods." Soon after, rebel columns began to emerge from the trees row after row of gray and butternut-clad soldiers. To the sergeant, they seemed unstoppable. Thomas turned slowly to an officer standing nearby and said simply, "Now you may give it to them, Captain." With that, "more than a dozen cannon, partly hidden 'til then in the roadside undergrowth, thundered to life, sending "charges of shot, shell, and canister tearing straight down the enemy's lines. Load after load, as fast as the artillerymen could handle, their pieces followed—a continuous shower of murderous iron. No troops on earth could stand that long, for they were taken at a disadvantage, could not reply, and were in an open field at point-blank range." Though the rebels made a manful effort to hold together, it did not take long for them to scatter back under the cover of the trees, leaving the wreckage of their dead and wounded behind them. Newton's carefully protected hilltop position held, but defenders of the Union center benefited from fewer natural advantages "where the long, east-west ridge . . . gradually lost elevation and dipped to a shallow valley."[130]

General George Maney's division of mostly Tennessee troops stood next in line to move against Thomas's Cumberlanders. They would run up against the Union

---

[128]   Bonds, *War Like the Thunderbolt*, 92.

[129]   Ibid., 93.

[130]   Bonds, *War Like the Thunderbolt*, 94-95; OR: I: XXXVIII: I, 298.

center defended by the division of Brigadier General William Thomas Ward, a "regular old Falstaff" known derisively as "Grandfather Ward" for his ineptness. Fortunately, his more-than-capable brigade commanders, most notably Colonels John Coburn and Benjamin Harrison, took the initiative that afternoon. Maney's 4,500-man division formed the heart of Hardee's corps and had a well-earned reputation as a hard fighting unit. It should have struck the hardest blow but instead "crept forward and barely fought at all." After running into the same heavy vegetation encountered by Walker, Maney failed to press forward; and fearing to advance blind, he halted and sent out skirmishers. His indecision killed the momentum of the Confederate assault. Bonds writes that "the contrast between their timid advance and the ferocious charges by rebels to the right and left of them is striking."[131] Despite solid effort along the rest of Hood's line by Alexander Stewart's corps, the day's fighting ended around 7:00 p.m. Though Hood eventually blamed Hardee for the day's lack of success, Maney and his four brigade commanders should have taken responsibility, but none of them submitted an official report explaining their lack of action. Modern estimates show that around two thousand Union troops and just over 2,500 Confederates fell as casualties at Peachtree Creek. The now-accepted Southern total stands in contrast to Sherman's inflated number of 4,796, long accepted by historians.[132]

Hood brought a numerically superior force to the point of battle. Five divisions, with two serving in support, contended against four Union divisions. Put another way, about twenty-three thousand rebels fought twenty thousand Yankees. On the field, Hood's commanders, most notably Hardee, let him down. The Georgian possessed four divisions yet got only Walker's into action. When Bate became separated, Hardee failed to get him back in line. Inexplicably, he also failed to use Cleburne's division which was positioned to fill in the gap left by Bate. Instead, Hardee held Cleburne in reserve, at the most important place in the attacking line, where Newton could have been flanked.[133]

All of this points to the sad state of Southern command by 1864. Too many seasoned officers had been lost, and those brought up to replace them lacked the requisite experience. Hardee should not bear blame by himself; after all, Cheatham's movement too far to the right had caused his hesitation and sent Confederate fortunes down the wrong path. Many Confederate problems that afternoon resulted from poor reconnaissance. Commanders found themselves unprepared for the difficult terrain that faced them. Here, "culpability probably rests on the shoulders of Major General Joe Wheeler. His cavalrymen had been skirmishing across Thomas's advance for days, and he was responsible for keeping

---

[131]   Bonds, *War Like the Thunderbolt*, 95-96.

[132]   Ibid., 106; McMurry, *Atlanta, 1864*, 152.

[133]   McMurry, *Atlanta 1864*, 151.

his commander informed of hour-by-hour developments."[134] Hood's plan possessed sound strategic elements and did not rely on simplistic frontal assaults. Davis writes that it was so good, "oblique assaults from the right by division, that Joe Johnston subsequently claimed credit for it."[135] Johnston, however, did not say this until he filed his official reports in October and still later in his memoirs. Davis states that no contemporary evidence has been found to support his case. In addition, such an attack was completely out of character for a man so fond of intricate defensive works.

Following the fighting on the 20th, Thomas remained within his entrenchments North of Atlanta, unsure of Hood's next move, and determined not to be caught off guard. During the course of the day, General McPherson marched rapidly toward the eastern edges of the city, and by that afternoon, he began throwing shells into Atlanta's center. Alarmed by this news, Hood ordered Hardee to send a division to extend Cheatham's line and help keep the Unionists at bay. Not having used Cleburne's veteran and hard-fighting infantry, which he had held in reserve, Hardee sent these men to fill the gap. While Cleburne moved rapidly and got into place, McPherson hesitated. Even though his twenty-five-thousand-man Army of Tennessee could have easily brushed Cheatham's corps, Wheeler's cavalry (now returned from Decatur), and Cleburne's division out of the way, something kept McPherson from going further. Perhaps it all seemed too good to be true that Atlanta stood so lightly guarded, or perhaps he suspected another Confederate trick. Whatever the reason, Mac's men remained immobile in the late afternoon, content to conduct artillery practice into the city's streets and terrorize what civilian population remained.[136]

McPherson's left flank stood exposed; in military terms, "in the air." Earlier, Sherman had sent Kenner Garrard's cavalry, which had guarded that position, on a four-day railroad-busting raid beyond Decatur. The Union commander took seriously Grant's warning back in July that Lee might use the Georgia railroad to reinforce the Army of Tennessee "with possibly twenty-five thousand troops."[137] Thus, rebel scouts found it possible to penetrate the area and discover McPherson's weakness. This news invited Hood to employ a daring attack reminiscent of the one made by Jackson on Hooker's exposed flank at Chancellorsville. There, Lee had boldly divided his army in the face of a superior enemy force, sending "Old Jack" on a secret march though wooded terrain. He surfaced in Hooker's rear, launching a devastating surprise assault while Lee hit the Yankee force from the other side.

Hood planned a similar deadly surprise for Sherman. He would send his most experienced general, Hardee, with his corps on a fifteen-mile night march to attack at dawn. According to Confederate reconnaissance, Hardee's men would

---

[134]   Davis, "A Reappraisal," in Savas and Woodbury, 62.

[135]   Ibid.

[136]   Bonds, *War Like the Thunderbolt*, 115; McMurry, *Atlanta 1864*, 152.

[137]   OR: I: XXXVIII, V, 149 & 209.

encounter only hospital tents and supply wagons on the Union left flank. When Hardee attacked, Hood planned for Cheatham and G. W. Smith, commander of the Georgia militia, to come out of the Atlanta entrenchments and catch McPherson in a vise. Alexander Stewart's corps had the task of keeping Thomas from coming to McPherson's aid. As Hood put it, "I determined . . . to attack the extreme left of the Federals in rear and flank and endeavored to bring the entire Confederate army into united action."[138] Instead of attacking well-prepared, entrenched enemy troops, Cheatham's men would assault Union soldiers confused and panicked by a surprise attack on their rear.

Students of the Civil War have often underestimated Hood's battles around Atlanta, allowing their judgments to be too heavily influenced by his actions at Franklin. Because of this, they tend to see him as "old-fashioned" or "inflexible," a man yearning for the glories of the straight ahead charge at Gaine's Mill. In truth, however, his tactics around Atlanta reveal imagination and creative intelligence. His plan for July 22 has been referred to by various historians as "brilliant in its conception," "Lee-like in its boldness and sweep," "a plan worthy of Lee," and "conceptually bold, [representing] the kind of Confederate assault that had broken Federal armies in the past."[139]

Hood endeavored to conceal his intentions and confuse the enemy by having the troops of Cheatham, Stewart, and Smith pull back into newly constructed lines behind the original city fortifications. Historian Stanley Horn writes that this "maneuver completely befuddled Sherman" who became convinced that the Confederates had retreated entirely from Atlanta. From his headquarters, Sherman now saw lines of empty fortifications previously bustling with rebel soldiers and activity. A somewhat ironically worded telegraph message from Cipher operator Major J. C. Van Duzer, however, to his counterpart in Washington, Major Thomas T. Eckert, described the situation at 9:00 p.m. on July 22:

> At daylight today, it was found that the rebels had gone from entire front, and General Sherman announced the occupation of Atlanta by Schofield and ordered pursuit by Thomas and McPherson. Vigorous pursuit was made, and the enemy was found in the fortifications of Atlanta and not Schofield.[140]

---

[138]   Hood, *Advance and Retreat*, 173.

[139]   Horn, *Army of Tennessee*, 354; Stephen Davis, *Atlanta Will Fall: Sherman, Joe Johnston, and the Yankee Heavy Battalions* (Willmington, Del: SR Books, 2001), 137; Albert Castel, *Decision in the West: The Atlanta Campaign of 1864* (Lawrence: University Press of Kansas, 1992), 379; Thomas B. Buell, *The Warrior Generals: Combat Leadership in the Civil War* (New York: Three Rivers Press, 1997), 372,

[140]   Horn, *The Army of Tennessee*, 354; OR: I: XXXVIII: V, 232.

"Old Woodenhead," as Lost Cause artists would later dub General Hood, was about to prove himself a formidable adversary.

McPherson could not get over a gnawing feeling of foreboding. He felt sure that July 22 would see one of the worst battles of the campaign and felt especially uneasy about his exposed flank. To ease his anxiety and give his army added protection, McPherson ordered General Grenville M. Dodge to send over the division of Thomas W. Sweeny to cover the unprotected position. To get official clearance for this, McPherson sent notification to Sherman "who promptly disagreed," replying by courier that he would prefer that Dodge's entire corps occupy itself with destroying railroad "back to and including Decatur." At that, McPherson rode to Sherman's headquarters to appeal the decision in person. Following discussion, the commanding general agreed that caution would be the best course when dealing with what he considered to be an "undoubtedly . . . brave, determined, and rash man."[141] McPherson's prescience would save Sherman's army and its commander's reputation from disaster.

Hardee's night march went off on schedule, but his corps arrived several hours late to start the battle on time. To avoid detection, the route headed out of Atlanta in a southeasterly direction for nearly six miles. The path then changed abruptly, heading North past Cobb's Mill. During this time, and at Hardee's discretion, Wheeler's cavalry would peel off and head for their raid on Union supply trains in Decatur. After clearing the mill, the gray columns split; Maney and Cleburne followed the Flat Shoals Road while Walker and Bate's divisions marched up the Fayetteville Road for about a mile before taking a forest track into a wilderness of undergrowth and forest, aiming at what they hoped would be the exposed end of McPherson's line. Here, it should be said that the task Hood had given Hardee and his men proved much harder than that taken by Stonewall Jackson who had marched by day with the help of reliable guides. Hood commented later upon the difficulties at hand:

> To transfer after dark our entire line from the immediate presence of the enemy to another line around Atlanta, [Cheatham, Stewart, and Smith] and to throw Hardee, the same night, entirely to the rear and flank of McPherson—and to initiate the offensive at daylight, required no small effort on the part of . . . men and officers.[142]

Hardee's route also contained three more miles than had Jackson's.

Inadequate reconnaissance and tough terrain caused Hardee to be delayed by about six hours. The Confederates finally found themselves ready to attack at about 12:30 p.m. rather than at daylight as hoped. Maney arrived, not on McPherson's

141   Bonds, *War Like the Thunderbolt*, 143.
142   Hood, *Advance and Retreat*, 174-175.

flank, but rather facing the enemy front near the point where the Union line elbowed East. Cleburne, on his left, and who'd cleared the forest last, providentially faced a gap between Dodge's newly arrived 16th corps and the 17th of Francis Blair. Walker and Bate, on Cleburne's right, the first to emerge from the heat absorbed tree line, unexpectedly encountered the veteran divisions of Fuller and Sweeney.

That Hardee arrived late made little difference to Union surprise. The clear, beautiful day had been quiet and oppressively hot. Blue clad men and officers lazed quietly, unaware of the rebel host creeping toward them from the shadows of the forest. McPherson and two of his division commanders, Generals Logan and Blair, having finished their midday meal, sat quietly smoking cigars under the shade of the trees.[143] Suddenly, a single gunshot rang out, sounding especially loud in the still afternoon air. This was followed by a rapidly escalating rattle of musketry. The shot that startled lounging Union generals into action may have been the one that killed Confederate General William H. T. Walker as he emerged from the tree line along the Federal far right. "Old Shot Pouch" or "Fighting Billy," despite accumulating bullets in his body dating back to the Seminole War of 1837, had finally run out of luck.

Bate and Walker's divisions went forward with a shout but found themselves rebuffed by stiff resistance from Dodge's corps. The Confederate plan to round the Union flank and rear appeared to have failed. Next in line, however, came Cleburne's veterans who quickly penetrated the gap between Blair's 17th corps and Dodge's 16th. Here, Unionists retreated in confusion as the rebels poured forward. Meanwhile, unaware of this new danger, General McPherson and some of his staff rode into the area thinking it still under their control. Within minutes, the young commander of the Army of the Tennessee lay dead after attempting to escape surrounding rebels.

Sherman, who had been confident that no Confederate attack would occur that day, experienced shock, both at Hardee's attack and by the sudden death of his protégé, James Birdseye McPherson. He later told General John "Black Jack" Logan, now in temporary command, that the Army of the Tennessee had the men to hold Hood from further advance and that he expected him to do it. By this time, however, "Cleburne's attack had carried three lines of works and swept northward, driving hundreds of fleeing blue solders back toward the linchpin of the Federal position: the high ground of Bald Hill."[144] As Confederate General George Maney's division ground forward on Cleburne's left and into the now disturbed Union front, the Federal divisional commander placed at the scene, Brigadier General Mortimer Legget, soon found himself assailed on both sides. Remarkably, however, hard fighting of Union troops positioned on the high ground combined with

---

[143]   Bonds, *War Like the Thunderbolt*, 144.

[144]   Bonds, *War Like the Thunderbolt*, 155.

Confederate weariness caused the position to stabilize. Sam Watkins recalled the fierceness of fighting around Bald Hill:

> We gave one long, loud cheer and commenced the charge. [Maney's division] As we approached their lines like a mighty inundation of the river Acheron in the infernal regions, Confederates and Federals meet. Officers with drawn swords meet officers with drawn swords, and man to man meets man to man with bayonets and loaded guns. The continual roar of battle sounded like unbottled thunder.[145]

Historian Russell Bonds writes that Hardee's men "had been marching and fighting with meager rations and almost no sleep for the past two days. Despite the flank attack, the gap in the line and the Rebel foray into the Federal rear, the Yankees held the line anchored on Bald Hill."[146]

Confederate cavalry also experienced incomplete success. Joe Wheeler's cavalrymen reached the outskirts of Decatur around noon, and immediately went into action. At first, the defending Union force, an infantry brigade commanded by John D. Sprague, got the better of the rebels' straight-ahead charge. Wheeler, however, changed tactics, hitting the Yankee's in flank and rear to drive them from position. Confederate loyalist and Decatur resident Mary Gay exulted over the rebel victory. "I had seen a splendidly equipped army ignominiously flee from a little band of lean, lank, hungry, poorly-clad Confederate soldiers, and I doubted not an over-ruling Providence would lead us to final victory."[147] Not long after achieving this success, however, Wheeler found himself called back to Atlanta by Hardee, wanting additional help. Though the cavalrymen could claim victory for driving Sprague from the field, the Union officer would get credit for saving most of McPherson's wagon train which he had earlier moved to a position of safety.

At around 4:00 p.m., Hood ordered Cheatham's corps forward, and soon the Tennessean's men punched a two-division sized hole in the Union center, clearly visible from Sherman's headquarters. Up to that time, the Union chieftain had been content to let his former command, the Army of the Tennessee, fight it out alone. This latest threatening development, however, changed his perspective. Quickly, Sherman ordered Schofield to bring his artillery to high ground overlooking the battlefield, and it began pounding Cheatham's lines. Sherman had had enough; first, the loss of McPherson, and now, a real threat to the honor of his old fighting force caused him to take things personally. The fire, directed by Sherman himself, proved mercilessly accurate, knocking holes in the Confederate lines and causing

---

[145]   Sam Watkins, *Company Aytch, or, A Side Show of the Big Show* (New York: Plume Books), 154.

[146]   Bonds, *War Like the Thunderbolt*, 159.

[147]   Mary A. H. Gay, *Life in Dixie During the War*, 4th ed. (Atlanta: Foote & Davies, 1901), 139-140, in Russel S. Bonds, *War Like the Thunderbolt*, 161.

Hood's final assault to lose momentum. As it had earlier at Bald Hill, fighting soon sputtered to a stop. With darkness, the rebels pulled back to their starting positions, and an uneasy silence settled over the lines.

Though promising in concept, Hood's attack most critically lacked coordination, causing the battle to be fought in piecemeal fashion. First, Bate and Walker's divisions went into action. After their repulse, Cleburne struck, exploiting the gap between two Union corps, but his troops fought for nearly an hour before Maney's division joined the fray. After impetus faded around Bald Hill, Cheatham finally joined in. Had these units been able to advance simultaneously (an extremely difficult thing to do), Hood may have achieved success in breaking McPherson's army. Sherman recognized his good fortune in an after-action report, remarking that "fortunately, their attacks were not simultaneous."[148]

In spite of failing in their ultimate objective, Hood's men had many positives to reflect upon. According to historian Stephen Davis:

> The assault on July 22 rocked Sherman's army, giving it the most brutal treatment of had received since leaving Chattanooga. The southerners inflicted almost 4,000 Union casualties (the Federals' largest single-battle loss of the entire campaign); killed Maj. Gen. James McPherson (the only Union army commander killed during the War); overran two division-lengths of enemy works, and captured twelve pieces of artillery. These gains could have been much more decisive if Hood's flank march had unfolded as he had intended it.[149]

Hood later wrote:

> Notwithstanding the non-fulfillment of the brilliant result anticipated, the partial success of that day was productive of much benefit to the army. It greatly improved the morale of the troops, infused new life and fresh hopes, arrested desertions . . . defeated the movement of McPherson and Schofield upon our communications in that direction, and demonstrated to the foe our determination to abandon no more territory without at least a manful effort to retain it.[150]

---

[148] OR: I: XXXIIX: I, 73.

[149] Stephen Davis, "A Reappraisal," in Savas and Woodbury, 64.

[150] John B. Hood, "The Defense of Atlanta," in *Battles and Leaders*, Vol. 4 (New York: The Century Co., 1884, 1888, 341. This article is a condensed version of what Hood wrote in *Advance and Retreat*, which was published by General Beauregard on behalf of the Hood Orphan Memorial Fund, New Orleans, 1880.

Following the explosive events of July 22, Sherman created another plan to pry the Confederates out of Atlanta. Rejecting an attack upon the city's fortifications as too costly and possibly unsuccessful, the Union commander opted for a strike at rebel communications South of the Georgia capital. By swinging the Army of the Tennessee, now with Oliver O. Howard at the helm in a westward arc from the position East of the city, Sherman could then extend his reach South and cut off the Macon railroad, Hood's last remaining supply link with the Confederacy. The rail line extended through East Point about three miles below rebel fortifications and from there to Montgomery, Alabama, and beyond. Once it had been severed, Sherman believed Hood would be forced to leave the city. To distract the Confederate commander, Sherman launched a massive cavalry raid extending beyond Decatur. Thus, on the night of July 27 Howard marched his new command as silently as twenty thousand men can march behind Schofield's army of the Ohio and Thomas's Cumberlanders. Federal cavalrymen filled in along Howard's now empty entrenchments.[151]

Sherman's clandestine movement did not remain so for long. Not only had Hood anticipated such a plan, but his scouts soon informed him of Howard's movement. In response, he countered with a march of his own, sending his former corps, now commanded by General Stephen Dill Lee, newly arrived from Mississippi, down the Lick Skillet Road to interpose itself between Howard and the railroad. Hardee stretched out his lines to fill in the gap left by Lee on Atlanta's East side so that things would appear normal to the Federals. Alexander Stewart, with an additional division on loan from Hardee, followed Lee. Hood's plan called for Lee to stall the enemy long enough for Stewart to "swing around to the West and North on July 29 [and] to strike and crush the right flank of the line which, Hood assumed, the Unionists would have established on the 28th when they found their southward progress blocked by Lee."[152] Lee had been specifically instructed not to attack unless attacked first and then only the Union right flank.[153] Here, it must be emphasized that Hood clearly told Lee not to attack fortified Federal troops.[154]

Howard arrived at the crossroads above East Point on the Lick Skillet Road first. Despite being told by Sherman that there would be no Confederate attack, Howard argued for caution and for Sherman's approval to lay out his lines in a mutually defensive manner. His men entrenched and fortified their lines, even using pews from a nearby Methodist meeting house known locally as Ezra church. Howard's precautions took time and may have kept him from reaching the railroad but would make a big difference to Union fortunes on July 28. Thus, within the space of a week, the intuition of two of Sherman's generals, McPherson and Howard,

151   McMurry, *Atlanta 1864*, 156.
152   McMurry, *Atlanta 1864*, 156.
153   OR: I: XXXVIII: V, 919.
154   Stephen Davis, "A Reappraisal," in Savas and Woodbury, 66.

ironically commanding the same army, saved the Union from embarrassment and heavy loss.[155]

When Lee encountered Federal troops around the Lick Skillet Road on the afternoon of the 28th, Hood's plans quickly went awry. Impetuously, the South Carolinian decided to launch a series of frontal assaults despite clear instruction not to do so. If Lee can be defended for his disobedience, it could be argued that the dense, heavily wooded terrain made clear view of the Union position impossible and that he had no idea that he was attacking an entire Army. Stewart came up, saw that Lee needed help, and joined in. By the time the battle of Ezra Church ended that afternoon, three thousand gray and butternut-clad bodies lay among the trees and underbrush, either dead or wounded. On the other side, casualties stood at a comparatively light 732. Castel remarks that though "historians . . . [often] blame Hood for this slaughter, the true culprit is Stephen Lee."[156]

Hood's object had been to delay Union advance on the railroad and then damage Howard badly enough to cause Federal retreat. Had Lee been more prudent, entrenching his men upon encountering the enemy, while using the terrain to his own advantage, that goal could have been realized. Stewart, then, not feeling the need to join in Lee's fruitless assaults, could have carried out the rest of the Confederate plan the following morning. This episode points again to the poor state of Confederate command by 1864. Many Southern officers had been promoted beyond their abilities. "Indeed, on July 28, Generals Lee and Stewart combined had only five weeks of experience at the corps level."[157] Despite terrific (and unnecessary) losses, however, Hood's men had once again frustrated Sherman's plans. Ezra Church bought Confederates another month before losing their rail connection.

Sherman decided to make another thrust at the railroad. Following Ezra Church, his troops tried for several days to locate the end of Hood's defensive line that protected Confederate communications. Not finding it by August 7, and becoming frustrated, Sherman pondered four options: (1) continue extending the right of his line in hopes of locating the rebel left, whereupon he could swing around it and cut off the eastern secessionist link to the outside world; (2) send the Army of the Tennessee on a wide flanking move to discover the end of Hood's left; (3) move his entire army group in a grand maneuver southward, flanking Hood's position, a strategy reminiscent of Union successes at Dalton, Marietta and Allatoona, forcing Hood to either attack or retreat; and (4) to keep pressure on the Confederates while resting Union soldiers for a big push around Hood's end by hitting Atlanta with an artillery bombardment—this last in hopes it might cause Hood to evacuate the city. Sherman decided on the fourth option, stating to Howard on August 10, "I

---

[155]   Albert Castel, *Decision in the West*, 424-425.

[156]   McMurry, *Atlanta 1864*, 157; Castel, *Decision in the West*, 435.

[157]   Davis, "A Reappraisal," in Savas and Woodbury, 66.

want to expend four thousand heavy rifle shots on the town before doing anything new and then will be prepared to act quick."[158] By acting "quick," Sherman referred to his developing plan—to use the full weight of the entire army to move below and around Hood's defenses and decisively destroy Hood's railroad somewhere in the vicinity of Jonesboro to the South. Before taking such action, however, the Union commander knew that his army needed time to rest and prepare. An extended artillery barrage would provide opportunity for both.

Sherman had to work within sharply defined time limits. His huge army stood in real danger of running out of supplies: food for animals by September 1 and food for men by September 15.[159] The political situation also exerted great pressure. Outside of Farragut's success at Mobile Bay, Northerners had little to cheer about. A message from Grant sent on August 9 summed up the situation: "We must win, if not defeated at home."[160] With bloody stalemate in the East and marked lack of progress in the West, Lincoln's fortunes for the 1864 election appeared bleak indeed.

By August 25, Sherman had put his grand flanking move into motion and withdrawal of Union troops from long-established fortifications mystified the Confederates. While many wanted to believe that Sherman was at last retreating, some suspected a Yankee trick. Castel comments:

> Far from being deluded . . . into thinking that Sherman is retreating, as contemporary critical historians will subsequently charge, Hood realizes that Sherman is launching or is about to launch another large-scale flanking movement to the South. What Hood does not know . . . is exactly what Sherman intends to do, where, when, and how.[161]

Indeed, all the Confederate commander could do was keep his troops on notice for any emergency. A message to Seddon, sent on the 28th revealed that though Hood had kept well informed of Sherman's movements, he did not know where they would lead.[162]

Though Hood had long seen an attack on the Macon railroad near Jonesboro as a logical Union goal, he did not think that Sherman would get there by August 31 and with so much force. A parallel exists with Lee's situation at Petersburg. As in Virginia, Jonesboro represented a site that had to be held if the army was to continue to be supplied. Like Lee, when realization dawned upon him, Hood rushed troops to the threatened area during the small hours of August 30 and 31. He sent what amounted to two thirds of his army, S. D. Lee's and Hardee's corps, but they

---

[158]   OR: I: XXXVIII: V, 453.

[159]   Castel, *Decision in the West*, 467.

[160]   OR: I: XXXVIII: V, 433-434.

[161]   Castel, *Decision in the West*, 487.

[162]   OR: I: XXXVIII: V, 997.

found themselves facing overwhelming odds in the form of the entire Army of the Tennessee and Thomas's corps, two thirds of Sherman's much larger force. Hood felt compelled to keep Alexander Stewart's corps and the Georgia military within Atlanta's fortifications because he remained unsure about Schofield and elements of the Federal cavalry.

The start of the battle on July 31 thus saw Hood facing a similar situation to that of Lee at Petersburg. The crucial difference lies in the fact that the two sides played opposite roles. At Petersburg, June 17 to 18, Grant's troops engaged in a series of uncoordinated assaults against secessionists heavily entrenched. Union men found themselves brutally driven back, and the siege of Petersburg resulted. In the West, S. D. Lee and Hardee ran up against strongly fortified Federals and were soundly defeated on July 31 and September 1. Thus, Hood's army, its supplies suddenly choked off, had no choice but to abandon Atlanta.[163] Davis writes:

> For all his part, John Bell Hood had done all he could to save the city. Taking command of the Army of Tennessee when overpowering enemy forces [stood] at the outskirts of Atlanta, Hood's only option had been to try to save the city by seeking opportunities for advantageous attack and then striking hard. As we have seen, he did this in his three battles of July."[164]

The fall of Atlanta became a great symbol of defeat in the South. The city's loss virtually guaranteed Abraham Lincoln's reelection; it shattered Confederate hope for negotiated peace with a McClellan government and foreshadowed Union victory in the war. Remembering Hood's retreat on the night of September 1, Colonel George W. Adair stated that he felt part of "a sick crowd, sick in heart and mind . . . . There seemed nothing left but to surrender."[165] Southern hopes approached their nadir with a demoralized army fighting in a demoralized county. Confederate military leaders began to reach desperately for some plan that could bring success.

Hood retreated as far as Palmetto, south of the fallen city; and the opposing legions drew back from their struggles to regroup. During this period, just about everything was in short supply, including officers. Combat losses caused many regiments and brigades to come under the command of inexperienced men. Mere promotions could not replace leadership lost. The resulting deficit haunted the Tennessee army for the remainder of its existence.

Hood sensed depression settling over his men and, casting about for ways to improve morale, wrote the Quartermaster-General in Richmond requesting that "funds for payment of this army should be sent without delay to [help] prevent

---

163   Davis, "A Reappraisal," in Savas and Woodbury, 78.

164   Ibid.

165   Time-Life Books, eds., *Atlanta* (Alexandria: Time-Life Books, 1995), 138.

dissatisfaction and desertion."[166] Indeed, the specter of desertion hovered over all Southern armies at this point in the war. Something needed to be done to stimulate hope; in desperation, Hood wrote Braxton Bragg requesting that General Lee send him his old division. Submerged in problems of his own negative situation, the general imagined that the Virginia troops still possessed their former esprit de corps and that they would inspire his men. Unfortunately, however, Lee faced depressingly similar morale problems in the East.[167]

Another factor affecting morale involved Hood's rancorous dispute with his senior corps commander, General William Hardee. Like Johnston, "Old Reliable" had the affection of his men and popularity with many officers in the army. Hood blamed Hardee for some of the failures around Atlanta, and Hardee in turn questioned Hood's fitness for command. In the end, Jefferson Davis, a friend of the Georgian, solved the immediate problem by assigning him to the department of Georgia, South Carolina, and Florida. Major General Benjamin Franklin Cheatham filled Hardee's position as corps commander and though an able officer, lacked the older man's experience. This single change in command hierarchy would have disastrous effect during the ensuing campaign in Tennessee.[168]

It might be expected after Atlanta's disastrous result that Davis might have relieved Hood and sent him to some quiet backwater to finish off the war. The proud president, however, did not give in to cries for the return of "Uncle Joe" and retained the general he had placed in command. His abiding hatred of Johnston could never have allowed such a turnabout, and humble pie did not form a part of the lean president's menu. In a report written in February of 1865, Davis admitted that he had given in to political pressure when he placed Johnston in command and declared that he had long known that the general "was deficient in enterprise, tardy in movement, defective in preparation, and singularly neglectful . . . of preserving our means of supply."[169] What he may have really been saying is that Johnston had powerful allies within the Confederate Congress and that he did not have the stomach to stand up to them. Instead, the president tried to quiet clamoring voices by taking another course. Like many compromise measures, however, it failed to satisfy everyone and ill-feelings continued to seethe just below the surface in the Army of Tennessee.

In consultation with Bragg and General Lee, Davis came up with a plan for creating an "overseer" for Hood, a more experienced general to advise him on future operations. One wonders how much Hood resented this; it amounted to almost being placed on probation. This function fell to Pierre Gustav Toutant Beauregard, "hero of Manassas," yet another military leader with whom Davis shared mutual

---

[166]   McMurray, *John Bell Hood*, 154-155.

[167]   Thomas Robson Hay, *Hood's Tennessee Campaign* (Dayton: Morningside, 1976), 21.

[168]   Hay, *Hood's Tennessee Campaign*, 23-24.

[169]   OR: I: XLVII: II, 1309.

feelings of disdain. To the president, bringing in Beauregard represented a more palatable alternative than bringing back Johnston. Though Beauregard could take over command in an emergency, he functioned mainly as a consultant.[170]

Davis visited the western army in order to ascertain its condition. The depletion of its officer corps, the run-down appearance of the men, and the widespread lack of shoes, clothing, and equipment shocked him. In consideration of the army's relative weakness compared with the Union forces, it was decided to avoid open battle while doing as much as possible to disrupt Sherman's vulnerable supply line. The Confederate command hoped thereby to draw Sherman out of Atlanta and distract him from further incursions into Georgia.

During his journey to Palmetto, the Confederate president inadvertently contributed to Union intelligence. En route to Hood's army, he stopped at Macon and delivered a speech in which he revealed plans for Sherman's supply line, a costly indiscretion on his part. Sherman later referred to Davis's remarks as "a very significant speech" and remarked that "Davis seemed to be perfectly upset by the fall of Atlanta, and to have lost all sense of reason . . . . He made no concealment of [his] vainglorious boasts, and thus gave us the full key to his future designs."[171] This occurred on September 24. And on the following day, while taking a morning ride with General Hood to inspect the army, Davis received indication that morale remained a serious problem. While some units voiced enthusiasm for the way ahead, others continued to cry out, "Give us Joe Johnston."[172]

During the evening, troops gathered to hear inspirational speeches given by officers and politicians. Sergeant Major S. D. Cunningham recalled, "a large assembly, a speaker's stand, and an attractive arrangement of battle flags."[173] He also noted that "a collection of burning pine knots gave a bright light and [that] a number of the best bands in army furnished fit music for . . . entertainment of our chief executive, military heroes and statesmen."[174] As part of his speech, Davis emphasized the large number of Tennesseans in the army and told them that their feet would soon be pressing the soil of their native state. Content such as this stimulated hope among the tired men who began to feel positive about what lay ahead. Davis's "pep talk" worked; there is nothing like the prospect of returning home after a long absence to arouse enthusiasm.[175]

Unfortunately, the president once again found opportunity to reveal Confederate strategy to the enemy. Unionists among the crowd in Augusta on September 27

---

[170] Hay, *Hood's Tennessee Campaign*, 28-29.

[171] William T. Sherman, *Memoirs of General William T. Sherman, By Himself*, Volume II (Bloomington: Indiana University Press, 1957), 141.

[172] Hay, *Hood's Tennessee Campaign*, 28-29; Hood, *Advance and Retreat*, 253.

[173] John A. Simpson, ed., *Reminiscences of the 41st Tennessee*, 86.

[174] Ibid.

[175] Ibid.

heard Davis declares, "We must beat Sherman, we must march into Tennessee . . . and push . . . the enemy back to the banks of the Ohio."[176] News of Davis's speeches helped Sherman formulate his own plans and expedite the "March to the Sea."

Though many Southerners must have sensed it, few soldiers or civilians would openly admit by the autumn of 1864 that the clock had struck midnight for the Confederacy. At Petersburg, the venerable General Lee stood motionless, his army locked in a death grip with the Union forces of U. S. Grant, while in the Trans-Mississippi, General Edmund Kirby Smith kept thousands of troops which could have been used elsewhere in virtual limbo. Atlanta had fallen, and the tide flowed away from the South. Yet despite such grim realities, one glimmer of hope winked in the twilight, and it burned within the ranks of Hood's tattered Army of Tennessee.

A bold and ambitious plan emerged from discussions between Davis, Hood, and Beauregard. It included crossing the Tennessee River, defeating Union forces present in the area, capturing Nashville with its wealth of supplies and the Federal base in the West, crossing the Cumberland River, and marching into Kentucky. Along the way, Hood's army, infused with victory, would gain strength from recruits eager to help in this final drive for Southern success. The triumvirate believed that Sherman would march toward Savannah but also felt that success in the Volunteer state would cause him to break off in Georgia and come in pursuit. Alternatively, should the Union army not strike for the sea but elect to follow Hood, the plan allowed for the possibility that his rejuvenated army would be able to defeat Sherman in a climactic battle somewhere in Kentucky. If the last proved true, Hood could then march through the Cumberland mountain passes, come in behind Grant, and relieve General Lee at Petersburg. Hood believed that if Sherman continued on to Savannah, he could win the race to support Lee two or three weeks before Sherman could aid Grant.[177]

Such an ambitious plan, though not impossible, contained an awful lot of "ifs." A myriad of logistical factors had to come together at the right time, and any one of these falling out of synchrony could spoil the overall result. Of ultimate importance was time itself. Though this conceptualization seems far-fetched now, chances of success appeared real as autumn winds blew across the landscape in 1864.

---

[176]   Hay, *Hood's Tennessee Campaign*, 23; OR: I: XXXIV: II, 540.

[177]   Hay, *Hood's Tennessee Campaign*, 55-56.

CHAPTER 3

The Road to Franklin

The months of October and November 1864 proved crucial for the military reputation and historical memory of John Bell Hood. After the fall of Atlanta, plans for further action developed in two stages. The first involved attacking and destroying as much of Sherman's supply line as possible. Hood aimed to begin North of the Chattahoochee River in order to draw the unionists away from the Gate City and pull them northward. This strategy offered a way to damage the federal troops and at the same time cause them to give up large swaths of territory gained during Johnston's tenure. Hood and his officers felt convinced that Sherman's men faced an acute supply shortage. The huge Union army of over ninety thousand with its horses, mules, wagons, and artillery, moved across the landscape like a large city. Confederates felt that if they had supply problems, so must Sherman. Thus, any threat to Yankee communications should elicit a quick and touchy response. In addition, Jefferson Davis felt great concern for Augusta, site of one of the South's last remaining powder works. If not *pushed*, Sherman must be *pulled* back. That the northern army did indeed have significant supply problems is indicated by a warning sent to the War Department in Washington from Colonel Amos Beckwith which stated succinctly that "Our supplies will soon be exhausted."[178]

Some critics might relate Southern plans in the wake of Atlanta too closely to the passive-aggressive policy followed by Johnston, but there are important distinctions. First, Davis specified highly aggressive action against Sherman's railroad, including not just random cavalry raids but infantry involvement as well. Second, the Confederate high command directed that after drawing Sherman close to Gadsden, Alabama, that a conclusive battle should be fought. In addition, Davis could be sure that Hood would fight not only because his personality differed so much from Johnston's but also because of what the president had seen in the Kentuckian's attempt around Atlanta.[179]

---

[178] OR: I: LII: I, 621, 698-699; Castel, *Decision in the West*, 467.

[179] McMurry, *John Bell Hood*, 158.

Davis, Hood, Beauregard, and Bragg developed the second stage, a more complex plan for achieving victory in the West, somewhat later. Here, Hood would cross the Tennessee River, attack and defeat the then small Federal force under Thomas at Nashville and then march northward through Kentucky toward the Ohio River or possibly through the mountain passes to Virginia to join General Lee. Confederate leaders assumed that victory at Nashville would inspire enthusiasm in the Blue Grass state and that Hood would gather recruits there by the thousands.

As will be discussed in detail later in this chapter, the plan depended upon lot of "ifs" as well as speed of execution and little room existed for error. As it developed, Hood spent three weeks waiting for supplies at Tuscumbia, Alabama, and once in Tennessee, severe weather and Yankee determination combined to allow half of Thomas's potential force, a twenty-thousand-man army under General Schofield, to elude rebel destruction. Hood tried to prevent Schofield from getting to Nashville by attempting to outflank him, first at Columbia and then at Spring Hill. At Spring Hill, a series of blunders and bizarre happenings allowed the unionists to escape Hood's well-conceived trap. Hood next found himself forced by time and circumstances to launch an ill-fated frontal assault against Schofield's troops at Franklin. This represented the Confederacy's last chance to prevent the Yankee army from reaching the Tennessee capital, only fifteen miles away. It is this battle which has come to define Hood's generalship and in large part dictate how he is remembered in history.

On September 29, Hood's men moved out of their camps at Palmetto to begin destruction of Sherman's supply line. In communication with the inspector general in Richmond, Hood described the action and its results: "Lieutenant-General Stewart's command succeeded in destroying completely some ten miles of the railroad." He further noted that "these operations caused the enemy to move his army, except one corps from Atlanta to Marietta, threatening an advance [on] our positions . . . not deeming our army in condition for a general engagement I withdrew it on the sixth of October to the westward."[180]

The first part of the plan appeared to be working. While avoiding significant contact with the Union force, the Confederates proceeded on an extended rampage against the railroad. Eventually, the path of destruction headed southwest toward Gadsden, Alabama. General Joe Wheeler's cavalrymen found themselves almost constantly engaged in rear guard skirmishing actions with pursuing blue troops.

Happy to be doing productive work and moving toward a crossing of the Tennessee, Hood found the morale and enthusiasm of his army much restored. As early as October 9, however, Sherman began to tire of the game as the disgruntled tone of a message to Grant reveals: "It will be a physical impossibility to protect the [rail] roads now that Hood, Forrest, and Wheeler, and the whole batch of devils are

---

[180]   OR: I: XXXIX: I, 802.

turned loose."[181] He went on to argue that a campaign of destruction by his army through Georgia would be more productive than chasing a "will o' the wisp" Hood. As he declared to Grant, "I can make the march, and I can make Georgia howl."[182] Army of the Cumberland historian Thomas Van Horne commented, "Although General Hood had not achieved the grand result which [Davis] had predicted, he had nevertheless been so far successful as to perplex the national commander and give hope to the insurgents." Van Horne further remarked that Hood "had moved in boldest disregard of railroad and communication . . . and in June, his northward march had been brilliantly executed."[183]

At this point, Grant remained skeptical of Sherman's idea, correctly believing that Hood headed for Nashville. He preferred that the Confederates be defeated before they got there. In the end, however, Grant left the final decision to Sherman; and on October 11, the western commander wired General Halleck in Washington, stating that he wished to leave Thomas to defend Tennessee while he conducted a march of destruction through Georgia to the coast. At that time, Sherman felt convinced that Hood would follow. Despite President Davis's September indiscretions, he did not know the entirety of the Southern plan. Had he been better informed, he would have realized that Hood had no intention of following him.

Critics argue that by letting Sherman go, the Confederate command failed to consider the devastating effects upon civilian morale that would result. Had the Southern plan proved successful, however, an offsetting boost in spirit would have resulted. Nashville, after all, had been under Union occupation since 1862, and its potential capture carried enormous symbolic importance. This would have been particularly true if its capture had been accompanied by Confederate advance into Kentucky.

For Hood, crossing the Tennessee River loomed as his immediate objective. In discussions with Beauregard, it had been decided to attempt this first at Guntersville, Alabama. At that point, however, both forces of nature and the nearness of Sherman conspired against success. One problem involved cavalry or rather, its scarcity. Since it had been decided that Wheelers's troops should continue to harass Union forces in Georgia, Hood looked to Nathan Bedford Forrest for support, but the "Wizard of the Saddle" was already in Tennessee and as yet in no position to help. Adding to his problems, consistently heavy rains left the river swollen and running fast, making a crossing at this point logistically impractical and dangerous. Beauregard, not on the scene, sent urgently worded messages urging Hood to cross the river at

---

[181]   OR: I: XXXIX: III, 162.

[182]   Ibid.

[183]   Thomas B. Van Horne, USA, *History of the Army of the Cumberland: Its Organization, Campaigns and Battles*. Written at the request of Major General George H. Thomas, Chiefly from his private journal and official and other documents furnished by him, Vol. II. (Cincinnati: Ogden, Campbell, & Co., 1875, reprint: Wilmington: Broadfoot Publishing Co., 1988), 167.

once. Frustrated and well aware of time's importance, the general could do nothing more than march further West to Tuscumbia and Florence in hope of finding more favorable conditions.[184]

Though morale continued to be strong, the army suffered from material degeneration and a consistent lack of food, clothing, and military supplies. Historian Albert Castel comments that morale revived not only because the army moved in a positive direction but also because of news about "Union setbacks in Virginia" and "increased war weariness in the North."[185] If barefoot privates marched in Sherman's army, they did not remain so for long, but a significant number of such unfortunates served in Confederate armies East and West at this point in the War. Men of all ranks had one loyal and constant companion: extreme fatigue. Sergeant-Major Sumner Cunningham remembered one Sunday "in which we *rested*, the men lay asleep nearly all day." He added that "the only ration issued was corn . . . one ear to four men. We roasted acorns and crab apples."[186] Such recollections bring to mind a mass of ill-clad gray and butternut scarecrows moving slowly but irrepressibly toward their rendezvous with fate.

Thus arrived the Army of Tennessee at Florence, Alabama, fittingly, it seems, on October 31, Halloween, for it would be haunted by the specters of failure and defeat. Engineers began immediate construction of a pontoon bridge with which to cross the river since Florence, like many mid-nineteenth century small towns, did not enjoy the luxury of a permanent bridge. Locals and travelers relied instead upon small ferries, not extensive enough to handle the needs of an army. Hood's regular requests for supplies went unanswered. Dire conditions, common to most Southern railroads and indicative of larger decay within the Confederate infrastructure, caused serious and, in Hood's case, fatal delays. On November 1, the Confederate Railroad Superintendent contacted Beauregard stating:

> I fear you have greatly overestimated the capacity and condition of this railroad to transport supplies to General Hood's army. Most of the bridges between here and Okolona were destroyed and recently only patched up to pass a few trains of supplies for General Forrest and are liable to be swept away by freshets which we may soon expect. The cross-ties are so much decayed that three trains ran off yesterday, and the track will be still worse in rainy weather. I have called upon General [Richard] Taylor for additional labor and will use every effort to forward the supplies . . . .[187]

[184]   Hay, *Hood's Tennessee Campaign*, 59.
[185]   Castel, *Decision in the West*, 484.
[186]   Simpson, *Reminiscences of the 41st Tennessee*, 91.
[187]   Hood, *Advance and Retreat*, 271-272.

For nearly a month, Hood's men waited for supplies of all kinds; although soldiers welcomed the rest, delay ultimately proved fatal to their success. It gave Thomas at Nashville much needed time to assemble and prepare an army capable of dealing with Hood's veterans. In preparing for his march to Savannah, Sherman stripped the Army of the Cumberland which Thomas had commanded since the removal of General Rosencrans after Chickamauga down to a skeleton force including its cavalry. This left "Old Pap" with pieces of various armies and green replacements. Hood's long delay at Tuscumbia gave the Virginian Unionist much needed time to prepare for the enemy arrival at the gates of Nashville.[188]

Hood has been attacked by contemporary historians for not crossing immediately into Tennessee, but this criticism ignores the fact that severe autumn storms and previous Union presence made movement into potentially barren country by an army of thirty thousand a risky proposition. As noted above, Hood's men lived on meager rations, and many lacked basic clothing and shoes. Historian Winston Groom writes of "the gaunt, hunger-glistening eyes of the ragged soldiers" and further notes that "shoes had a predictable life span . . . after the 250-mile march from Atlanta that span had long ago run out."[189] At the very least, in waiting to resupply, Hood showed consideration for the welfare of his troops.

The idea of returning to Georgia to oppose Sherman had been considered, but a head start of over two hundred miles made it impossible for weary Confederates to catch the Union forces. Added to this difficulty, such a retrograde movement could have been seen by many as yet another retreat. Desertion, already a serious problem, would have increased, especially among men from Tennessee, causing a large portion of Hood's army to simply melt away. Equally important is the fact that Sherman's advance had systematically stripped the country over which Southern troops would have to travel. Moreover, Hood knew that if he returned to Georgia, Thomas would be left free to descend into Alabama. By sending the army so far West, Davis, Hood, and Beauregard had committed it to one option, the march to Nashville and Kentucky.

On November 20, the army moved forward at last. Alexander Stewart's Corps crossed the wide river first, and the rest of the Confederate host followed the next day. Newly supplied and rested, men marched toward the state line eagerly. Tennessean Sam Watkins remembered how "every pulse did beat and leap and how every heart did throb with emotions of joy."[190]

---

[188] Benson Bobrick, *Master of War: The Life of General George H. Thomas* (New York: Simon & Schuster, 2009), 266-67; Frank A. Palumbo, *George Henry Thomas: The Dependable General* (Dayton: Morningside House, Inc., 1983), xi.

[189] Groom, *Shrouds of Glory*, 228.

[190] Sam Watkins, *Company Aytch* (New York: Penguin Putnam, 1989), 214. This was originally published in Nashville by the Cumberland Presbyterian Publishing House in 1882.

To facilitate movement of so large a force on limited roads, Hood's army traveled in three separate columns. Taking the longest route, Major General Benjamin Franklin Cheatham, known simply as "Frank" to most soldiers, led his men up through Waynesboro. The shortest journey belonged to Alexander, "Old Straight," Stewart's troops, while the most difficult path fell to S. D. Lee who moved over rugged farm tracks ill-suited to carry thousands of men, wagons, and artillery. Every bit as poor as the roads, the weather tormented the ill-clad mass of humanity. Cunningham remarked that "progress was very slow, the artillery and wagons cutting through the mud almost to the hubs."[191] A freezing north wind penetrated clothing, and chilled fingers had difficulty holding rifles. Psychologically, the large number of Tennesseans within the ranks found it easier to endure such hard conditions because they were heading home. Even these men, however, encountered reminders of their stern purpose. Sergeant-Major Cunningham wrote that in nearing the state line, "we saw stretched over the road a white strip of cloth about a yard wide and four yards long on which these words were written: 'Tennessee's a grave or a free home'"[192] Protecting the flanks of slowly moving but resolute infantry, three columns of Forrest's cavalry drove away the small number of Union troops in the area. To outnumbered Union cavalry, commanded by Kentuckian General John Croxton, it seemed plain that something ominous was afoot.[193]

Though the invasion of Tennessee had begun, the fact remained that three significant delays had occurred, the last being most critical. Had Hood been able to get across the river on October 1, he would have encountered nothing between his army and Nashville. By the time the Southerners finally got underway, however, Thomas had a combined force of about twenty-seven thousand consisting of General David Stanley's 4th Corps, and the 23rd Corps of John Schofield. The senior officer would command the whole, stationed at Pulaski, sixty miles south of the capital. At this point, Hood's army numbered just under forty thousand, but unlike Thomas's, Hood's would receive no reinforcements.[194]

---

[191]   Simpson, *Reminiscences of the 41ˢᵗ Tennessee,* 92-93.

[192]   Ibid.

[193]   Colonel Henry Stone of Thomas's Staff in *Battles and Leaders of the Civil War,* Vol. 4 (New York: The Century Co., 1884, 1888), 443. The following quotation is taken from "Repelling Hood's Invasion of Tennessee." Major Henry C. Connelly of the 14th Illinois cavalry recalled an incident while guarding Capron's infantry during Hood's advance on Columbia: "While passing through a long lane south of Columbia, Forrest's forces charged the brigade in rear and on both flanks with intrepid courage. Our command was confined to a narrow lane with men and horses in the highest state of excitement . . . . The only thing that could be done was to get out as promptly as possible and before Forrest's forces should close in and capture the command." Also see OR: I: XLV: I, 1015.

[194]   Hay, *Hood's Tennessee Campaign,* 77-78.

General Schofield, unsure of enemy intentions, should have sensed potential danger. Hood kept him in the dark until the 24th. Poor visibility caused by bleak weather conditions, combined with communication problems, made it extremely difficult to know what was going on. On the 21st, Colonel Horace Capron stationed near Waynesboro, sent messages to Schofield indicating quiet conditions in the area. The general, more aware than he, warned sharply, "I expect to hear of the capture of your command. Move back at once toward Mount Pleasant . . . . Possibly, you may get this in time."[195]

Alert to potential danger, Thomas advised Schofield "to move back gradually from Pulaski and concentrate in the vicinity of Columbia," and in a message to Halleck expressed concern about the disparity in numbers: "Hood's force is so much larger than my present available force, both in infantry and cavalry, that I shall have to act on the defensive, Stanley's corps being only twelve thousand effective and Schofield's is ten thousand effective. As yet, General [James Harrison] Wilson can only raise about two thousand effective cavalry."[196] Thomas anxiously awaited arrival of ten thousand reinforcements under General Andrew Jackson Smith coming from Missouri and Wilson's cavalry from Kentucky. Despite Thomas's warning, however, Schofield delayed. He retained an erroneous belief that Hood would assail him at Pulaski and had not yet realized, as Thomas had, that the Confederates intended to get between him and Nashville with the goal of destroying his force.

By the twenty-second, Cheatham's Corps had traveled eighteen miles, and Forrest's cavalry had pushed their outnumbered Union counterparts to the Southwest. On the following morning, Hood's entire army converged near the recently deserted town of Waynesboro. A glance at the map reveals that rebel troops stood at that point only slightly above and West of Pulaski. Though Schofield had access to the most direct route, it would be a close race to Columbia.

Just after midnight, with November 24 being only a few moments old, Schofield finally ordered his generals to march their commands northward. Tired soldiers, rudely shaken from the cocoon of sleep, hurriedly gathered their equipment and formed into line. Almost as soon as the blue troops began to move, however, a seemingly clairvoyant Forrest began to harass the weary columns. Thus, the first glimmerings of dawn saw Schofield's army in hasty retreat.[197]

Once in Columbia's outskirts, Union soldiers hastened to set up defensive works. Captain Levi Scofield, with the 23rd Corp of Cox's division, recalled arriving soon after sunrise: "As we approached the town, well-kept farms and spacious lawns with long, straight lanes bordered with trees, leading up to . . . handsome mansions

---

[195]   OR: I: XLV: I, 964.

[196]   Ibid.

[197]   OR: I: XLV: I, 112, 357, 400, 1020.

gave us the impression of peace and comfort. But how quickly that was to change."[198] In sharp illustration, Scofield wrote of an incident that occurred as worn out blue cavalry arrived with Forrest's rebel troopers in hot pursuit: "A dashing captain on a splendid black charger with foam-flecked shoulders and a yellow saddle blanket was in advance, deliberately shooting our men in the back of their heads with his revolver. He was dropped from his seat . . . [however,] by the first infantryman that crossed the road."[199] Colonel Stone commented that the arrival of Jacob Cox's division had been just in time, adding that "in another hour Forrest would have been in possession of the crossings of Duck River, and the only line of communication with Nashville would have been broken."[200]

For three days, the situation in front of Columbia remained tense though stable, punctuated by intermittent skirmishing and musket fire. General Thomas began sending reinforcements to the beleaguered Schofield, and in an 8:00 a.m. message on the 27th declared "If you can hold Hood in check until I can get [General Andrew Jackson] Smith up, we can whip him."[201] But at 12:30 that afternoon, Schofield replied, indicating his concern that Hood intended to cross the Duck River "above Columbia and as near as he can."[202]

Grant's Chief-of-Staff, General Rawlins, had written Thomas that Smith's command of two divisions totaling fourteen thousand would leave Saint Louis by November 10. This promise was not fulfilled however, as Smith's men "had to march entirely across the state of Missouri; and instead of leaving Saint Louis on the 10th, he did not arrive there until the 24th."[203]

Schofield's force, too small to hold a line threatened by Hood's infantry numbering nearly forty thousand and Forrest's cavalry at around ten thousand, had to pull back across the river, destroy the railroad bridge, and scuttle its pontoon boats. Stone relates that "this was an all night job, the last of the pickets crossing at 5 in the morning [on the 28th]." He stated further that Schofield's "little army had been exposed day and night to all sorts of weather except sunshine and had been almost continually on the move."[204]

One wonders how much Grant in Washington regretted allowing himself to be swayed by Sherman's argument for a march through Georgia. After all, Grant had been convinced from the beginning that Hood's goal would be Nashville. Now Sherman, with the bulk of the Army of the Cumberland, a force of approximately

[198] Levi T. Schofield, *The Retreat from Pulaski to Nashville; Battle of Franklin, Tennessee, November 30, 1864.* (Cleveland: Press of the Caxton Co., 1909), 11.

[199] Ibid., 13.

[200] *Battles and Leaders,* Vol. 4, 443.

[201] OR: I: XLV: I, 1086.

[202] Ibid.

[203] *Battles and Leaders,* Volume 4, 443.

[204] Ibid., 444.

sixty thousand, advanced toward Savannah, meeting little opposition while events in Tennessee boiled toward a crisis, and Grant found it difficult to supply Thomas with much needed reinforcements. November thus proved laden with fatal import for Sherman. While it is true that the conquest of Atlanta had guaranteed the reelection of President Lincoln, the perceived success of his March to the Sea began to depend upon how well George Henry Thomas would be able to cope with John Bell Hood. At this time, Schofield's army represented over fifty percent of Thomas's effective troop strength; had it been isolated and forced to surrender, Union fortunes in the West would have become grave indeed.

On the evening of the twenty-seventh, with a storm whistling outside, General Hood and his generals gathered at Beechlawn, the stately home of Mrs. Amos Warfield for a council of war. There, in the flickering candlelight, they developed a plan. Since the enemy seemed to expect a direct assault to their front, Hood instead proposed a grand flanking movement, taking most of the army around and above Schofield in the direction of Spring Hill. He assigned Forrest the important task of driving Wilson's cavalry away which both protected Union flanks and kept leadership informed of Confederate movements. While these events unfolded, S. D. Lee's corps, along with the rest of the artillery, would demonstrate in front of Columbia to give the impression of impending attack. Sooner or later, Hood knew his old classmate would see through the deception and make a dash for Nashville. By that time, however, he hoped to have beaten Schofield to Spring Hill and blocked his retreat. When the Union troops moved out, Lee could move on their rear trapping them in a vise. The ensuing battle, Hood hoped, would result in Schofield's destruction and leave Thomas alone at Nashville.[205]

In cavalry action on the morning of the 28th, Forrest succeeded in separating Wilson from the rest of the Union army. Wilson had somehow become convinced that Forrest was headed for Nashville. By the end of the day, Union cavalry no longer factored into these opening movements, and Schofield became virtually blind. At 1:00 a.m. the following morning, the Union commander received an urgent message from Wilson stating that Hood's movements pointed directly at Franklin, only fifteen miles from the capital. Wilson declared that rebel infantry would cross the Duck sometime before dawn and urged Schofield to "get back to Franklin without delay, leaving a small force to detain the enemy."[206] The precarious nature of the situation apparently caused Wilson to ignore protocol, seemingly giving orders to his commanding general. Though Wilson had been physically maneuvered out of the way, he had not failed to grasp the nature of Hood's intentions.

Thus catalyzed, Schofield began preparation for a retreat toward Franklin yet paradoxically, continued to harbor doubts. A noisy S. D. Lee in his front made him wonder about an attack, and because of his doubts, he ordered General David

---

[205]   OR: I: XLV: I, 687.

[206]   OR: I: XLV: I, 1140.

Stanley "with two divisions, Wagner's and Kimball's, to Spring Hill, taking the trains and all the reserve artillery."[207]

He waited almost too long. Hood delayed crossing the Duck River because of high water and the late arrival of his pontoon train. He did not begin moving until around 7:30 a.m. but did so with a force of nineteen thousand men. Because of the need to deceive Schofield, the troops had to march cross country which caused arduous and slow progress. Private Edward McMorris of the First Alabama noted that the "line of march was over cultivated . . . open country [whose] high hills and dense cornstalks [presented] a serious impediment to our progress."[208] John Copely of the 49th Tennessee also commented that "we moved . . . over rocks, hills, down steep hollows, over stone and rail fences through thick underbrush as fast as possible . . . ."[209]

John Bell Hood, who some historians have portrayed as a clumsy proponent of the frontal assault, thus enacted a masterful flanking maneuver, the origins of which, it can be argued, trace directly to the thinking of Stonewall Jackson. Yet the weather, a factor beyond control of all generals, delayed Hood's advance. In this instance, it caused the attack to fail and would prove, not for the last time, to be one of Hood's most relentless enemies.

At 11:00 a.m., General Thomas sent Schofield a message recommending that he move away from Columbia, beyond Franklin, and retire to Nashville. With S. D Lee's artillery in front, booming in indication of a coming attack, Schofield, however, remained indecisive. He finally made up his mind in the early afternoon and instructed Stanley near Spring Hill to select a defensive position and await his arrival. Even so, Schofield's withdrawal did not begin until after four o'clock.[210]

Before noon, Stanley and Ruger's men began moving into Spring Hill. Because Union troops had sighted rebel cavalry, they knew that Forrest was lurking somewhere nearby. Local residents soon expressed displeasure at seeing Yankees. First Sergeant Smith of the 120th Indiana remembered the reception Union soldiers received as they passed a women's college. "The young ladies were out in force," he wrote, "we soon discovered that they were what the boys [called] she rebels . . . . They taunted us, hissed at us, and I do not know, but they would have spit at us if they could have held their tongues still long enough. They informed us that Forrest would shortly transfer us to the Southern Confederacy."[211]

Forrest made contact with the Union troops soon after they gained possession of the town, and in spite of repeated attempts, he could not dislodge them. The odds shifted heavily in Confederate favor however, when infantry led by Cheatham's

---

[207]   *Battles and Leaders*, 444.

[208]   Jamie Gillum, *The Battle of Spring Hill: Twenty-Five Hours of Tragedy* (Jamie Gillum, 2004), 23.

[209]   Ibid.

[210]   OR: I: XLV: I, 1139, 1141.

[211]   Joseph Edmunds, 120th Indiana, in Gillum, *The Battle of Spring Hill,* 27.

Corps began to arrive around three o'clock. Within two hours, nearly twenty thousand Southern troops would be aligned against about five thousand soldiers. By that time, the tardy Schofield had managed to get underway, but the timing would be close.

After crossing Rutherford's Creek, about two miles from Spring Hill, Hood ordered General Cheatham to "go [with his corps] take possession of and hold [the Columbia Pike] at or near Spring Hill. Accept whatever comes and turn all those wagons over to our side of the house."[212] He referred to the steady line of Union wagon traffic moving up the pike, a procession over seven miles long. Cheatham had Patrick Cleburne deploy his division along Rally Hill Pike facing East, less than one mile from its goal the Columbia Pike, Schofield's escape route to Nashville. Hood watched Cleburne advance and then rode back to get Cheatham. Not finding the Tennessean, he then ordered William B. Bate, also of Cheatham's Corps, to march his division east, seize the pike, and begin a sweeping movement toward Columbia. This attack, though initially successful against outnumbered infantry, stalled when it ran up against a strongly held artillery position at about four o'clock.[213]

As Cleburne regrouped and prepared for another attack, Cheatham arrived on the scene and ordered the Irishman to wait until John C. Brown's division could come up to support his right. Up to this point, the attack appeared promising, and Cleburne felt that another good thrust might finish the job, but delay, failing daylight, and fatigue made striking again problematic. "It was . . . near sunset, and being tired, we lay down at dusk in line of battle," recalled William Matthew's of Lowery's brigade.[214] Pat Cleburne, a proven hard fighter, could not understand the delay. In his opinion, enough troops remained on the field to deal with the enemy. As they waited for General Cheatham's return and the anticipated order to resume their assault, Captain Dinkins of Chalmer's Cavalry division recalled a conversation between Cleburne and General Chalmers. Cleburne remarked, "They are badly paralyzed. I rode to within fifty yards of their works without danger."[215] Chalmers then tried in vain to get Brown to join Cleburne in resuming the attack. Near enough to overhear the conversation, Captain Dinkins later recalled that Brown "very curtly" answered that he had no orders. Chalmers, irritated at Brown's tone, countered, "General, when I was circumstanced as you are at Shiloh, I attacked without orders."[216] The beleaguered Brown also faced questions about his reluctance to move from Captain H. M. Neely of General John C. Carter's staff. In response to Brown's dogged insistence that he had no orders, Neeley remarked that "if he

212   OR: I: XLV: I, 1170.
213   Ibid.; Eric Jacobson, *For Cause and Country,* 119-120.
214   Gillum, *The Battle of Spring Hill,* 117.
215   Ibid.
216   Diary of Harold Young, *Confederate Veteran* 16, p.34, and Brown's statement in the *Southern Historical Society Papers* 9, p. 538, in Jacobson, *For Cause and Country,*154.

would take the responsibility of beginning the attack . . . he could safely count on a new feather in his cap as it would be a quick and easy matter to capture and destroy Schofield's corps in its present condition."[217] Moreover, frustration at the failure to attack spilled over into the enlisted ranks. Colonel Ellison Capers of the 24th wrote that the troops "were in momentary expectation of moving" and "could not understand why we did not attack, and every man felt, and I heard hundreds of remarks that for some cause we were losing a grand opportunity."[218] In an 1885 letter written to Capers, Union Colonel John Lane, commander of the second brigade of Wagner's division who faced Brown at Spring Hill, supported the argument that the Confederates had permitted a superb chance to slip away. Lane stated that "in your front, covering at least a mile, there were fewer than five hundred men to resist your veterans."[219]

Meanwhile, with darkness coming on and the seemingly interminable delay continuing, Schofield's men continued to move hurriedly up the Columbia Pike virtually unchallenged. At long last, at about 4:45 p.m., Cheatham returned. He had been searching for General Bate to add more weight to the attack. Hood had ordered that general to seize the pike earlier. Not finding Bate but seeing Cleburne and Brown waiting, he ordered them to resume the attack. As soon as Brown got his division into line, the attack was to go forward on the sound of his guns. The general quickly marched his men into position, threw skirmishers out, and made ready. In the dim light, he could just make out an enemy brigade in his front. Just as the troops were to go forward, however, Brown received a message from General Strahl warning that there were Union troops overlapping his line and that he was in danger of being flanked when the assault moved ahead. With this news, Brown hesitated and refused to move. Once again, everything came to a halt.[220]

In the dim light, it was difficult to discern the strength of the overlapping force. But what was actually being seen was a lightweight extension of the Federal left flank, consisting of a single regiment, the 100th Illinois and one company from the 40th Indiana. These were troops that would have been brushed aside by the weight of a Confederate division.[221]

While Cheatham continued to search for Bate, the opportunity to smash the Federals in front of Spring Hill began to disappear because time was running out. Cheatham contributed to the loss of a second opportunity when he finally found

---

[217]   Young Diary, *Confederate Veteran* 16, p. 35, in Jacobson, *For Cause and Country,*154-155; OR: I: XLV: I, 736.

[218]   Young Diary, *Confederate Veteran* 16, p.35, in Jacobson, *For Cause and Country,* 154-155.

[219]   Walter B. Capers, *The Soldier-Bishop Ellison Capers,* 112-113, in Jacobson, *For Cause and Country,* 154-155.

[220]   Sayers, Althea, *The Sound of Brown's Guns: The Battle of Spring Hill, November 29, 1864* (Spring Hill: Rosewood Publishing, 1995), 87-93.

[221]   Jacobson, *For Cause and Country,* 127.

General Bate. At a little past 5:00 p.m., Bate's sharpshooters, according to that general's official report, "deployed as skirmishers [were] within one hundred yards of and commanded the turnpike, checking the enemy's movement along it in my front, and my lines were being adjusted for a further forward movement . . . when I received orders from General Cheatham to halt and join my right to General Cleburne's left."[222] Incredulous, Bate initially refused, but when faced with a second order, he grudgingly complied. Thus, in the space of a single hour, two great opportunities had been squandered. By the time Bate found Cleburne's left, it was 9:00 p.m., and any hope of furthering the attack ended. General Bate gave an account of a meeting he had with Hood later that night in which he said, "I did not pass onto the turnpike and sweep toward Columbia as you had directed me to do because just at that time I received an order from . . . General Cheatham to halt and align my division with the left of Cleburne's."[223]

Additional mix-ups and delays followed. After General Cheatham discovered the problem on Brown's flank, he agreed that the attack should not go forward until more support could be found, and he sent for Alexander Stewart's Corps to support Brown. Earlier, two divisions had been enough to handle the Federals in the town; but at this point, Cheatham had added a third and wanted to compliment this with an entire corps.

Prior to all of this, Hood had ordered Stewart's Corps of about eight thousand men to march North of Spring Hill and set themselves astride the all important Columbia Pike, thus blocking Schofield's exit. It was the commanding general's understanding that by doing so, Stewart would partially overlap Cheatham's Corps. But Hood had not been informed that Cheatham had changed position in the meanwhile and that by this time, Brown's division actually angled away from the turnpike.[224]

Not long after Stewart began his northward movement, an irritated Hood confronted Cheatham with the question: "Why in God's name have you not attacked the enemy and taken possession of the pike?"[225] When Cheatham explained the situation involving Brown's flank and proposed that Stewart support him, the commanding general specifically asked if the turnpike would be covered. Cheatham assured him that it would. Hood's mood did not improve, but he sent a courier to redirect Stewart. As revealed above, supporting Brown's left would not cover the route being used by Union Troops.[226]

By 9:00 p.m., an exhausted General Hood retired to his headquarters under the impression that orders had been fulfilled; Schofield would be trapped and

---

[222]   OR: I: XLV: I, 742.

[223]   OR: I: XLV: I, 742.

[224]   Jacobsen, *For Cause and Country*, 144; Sayers, *The Sound of Brown's Guns*, 93.

[225]   Hood, *Advance ad Retreat*, 286.

[226]   Hood, *Advance ad Retreat*, 286.

dealt with on the following day. He retained this comforting illusion until visited by Forrest and Stewart, both of whom voiced concerns. It then became clear that he and Cheatham had been operating under different plans and that Cheatham had become so focused on the enemy directly in his front that he had seemingly forgotten about the main body moving up the road from the South. In his distracted state, Cheatham had pulled all available troops *back* from the pike in order for facilitate the battle around Spring Hill itself. Hood asked the two generals if either of them could do something about blocking the pike. Stewart voiced concern about how tired his men were, and Forrest complained about being low on ammunition. Tennessee Governor Isham Harris, present at the time, stated that Hood told Stewart to give the cavalrymen ammunition. Forrest said he would do the best he could.[227]

At about 10:00 p.m., the approximate time of the meeting between Hood and his generals, Edward Johnson's division moved into bivouac to the left of Bate. Meanwhile, the long line of Federal troops continued to march up the pike within less than two hundred yards of the Confederate army. Thomas McFarland of the 175th Ohio remembered a peculiar incident: "When we first saw the fires we were delighted at the near prospect of a rest, as we were very tired. When we came up the pike opposite the fires we were hailed with 'What regiment is that?' In answer Private Plummer replied, 'Alabama Tigers' and in turn inquired, 'What regiment do you belong to?' They gave the name of a Confederate regiment—the name and number . . . we took the hint and traveled."[228]

Though many were aware of the Yankees traveling up the pike, it took a humble, barefoot private to make his way to Hood's headquarters, sometime around midnight, to warn the general about what was happening. After hearing the man's story, Hood sent him to General Cheatham with orders to move on the pike and fire on the approaching blue troops. Cheatham, in turn, ordered Johnson's division to advance, something that tired and contentious general was loath to do. But in the end, both Cheatham and Johnson rode out to the pike at about 2:00 a.m. and found it empty. The tail end of Schofield's army had marched out of sight.[229]

In the end, the attack on Stanley's division was called off, yet the enduring question concerns who stopped it from going forward. Hood and Cheatham remembered things differently in postwar years. Hood claimed that he had no intention of ending the attack after his stormy meeting with Cheatham. Cheatham, however, specifically stated that "I was never more astonished than when General Hood had concluded to postpone the attack till daylight. The road was still

---

[227]   Jacobson, *For Cause and Country*, 160-161.

[228]   Gillum, *The Battle of Spring Hill*, 189.

[229]   Jacobson, *For Cause and Country*, 170-171.

open—orders to remain quiet until morning—and nothing to prevent the enemy from marching to Franklin."[230]

While a portion of the last sentence is true, the first part is doubtful. Subsequent attempts by Hood later that evening belie "orders to remain quiet until morning," and members of Hood's staff stated, "They personally delivered orders to Cheatham directing him to attack, and neither mentioned anything about the assault being called off."[231] Perhaps most damaging to Cheatham is the account given by Major Joseph B. Cumming who witnessed part of his meeting with Hood:

> General Hood sent me forward with an order to attack at once. I delivered the order, and as I had ridden hard to deliver it, I returned to General Hood's headquarters at a slow pace, expecting every minute to hear the sound of an attack on the pike. It was now getting dark. It was the twenty-ninth of November, chilly and drizzling. When I reached General Hood's headquarters, to my astonishment, I found General Cheatham there, he having outridden me by a different route. He was remonstrating with General Hood against a night attack.[232]

By combining the facts available, it appears unlikely that Hood would have agreed to abandon the attack; and in any case, he demanded that Schofield's escape route on the turnpike be sealed off.[233] It is likely Cheatham once again changed Hood's orders. Why did Cheatham race to Hood's headquarters when he had just been given specific orders to attack? The answer is probably that he had already set his mind against it. Maybe Cheatham thought the night assault was too dangerous, and he hoped to save lives. Historical hindsight reveals, however, that the Battle of Franklin, which occurred the following afternoon, stands as a bloody anticlimax to more costly failures at Spring Hill. Cheatham, despite his good intentions, was guilty of insubordination in the face of the enemy and should have faced arrest and court-martial. Hood, for his part, should have threatened Cheatham with such punishment and insisted his orders be carried out to the letter. This, perhaps, was his greatest mistake.

Since Forrest's cavalry raid on the pike failed to halt Union progress, why did he fail to inform Hood? If he had, Hood would, based upon his multiple orders to various officers to block the road, have tried something else. The mystery is why Forrest failed to send word to the commanding general. Taken at face value, this

---

[230] Cheatham, *Southern Historical Society Papers* 9, 526, in Jacobson, *For Cause and Country*, 170-171.

[231] Siebring and Hansen, ed., *Memoirs of a Confederate Staff Officer*, 61, in Jacobson, *For Cause and Country*, 143.

[232] Joseph Cumming, *Recollections*, 72, in Jacobson, *For Cause and Country*, 143.

[233] Jacobson, *For Cause and Country*, 144.

represents a terrible and irresponsible blunder, but perhaps no one bothered to inform Forrest, and he assumed that things had been taken care of. Here again, fatigue may have played a role. Hood, Forrest, Cheatham, and the mass of private soldiers experienced the numbing effects of exhaustion. Whatever the reason, and no definitive evidence has yet emerged to reveal what it was, Bedford Forrest has never been significantly criticized for his failure to close the pike and for not reporting it to Hood. Why? Perhaps, because in the post-war years dominated by the Lost Cause mythologists, Forrest joined Robert E. Lee as an unassailable Confederate icon.

The question of what General Hood was doing while significant events leading to the failure of his plan occurred should be addressed. Where was he, and why did he fail to see that his orders were not carried out? As commanding general, Hood had more to do than supervise Benjamin Franklin Cheatham, his second in command, a man he trusted. Hood's teachers had been Lee and Jackson. Lee taught him to delegate responsibility to subordinates, freeing him to concentrate on larger details, no shortage of which existed on that confusing afternoon. It is also important to remember that key events, Cheatham's halting Cleburne's attack on Stanley while seeking additional support, for example, and his pulling Bate away from the pike south of Spring Hill, took place in the space of a single hour. During that fatal period, the commanding general had responsibilities to attend to, such as setting up a central command center and checking on progress in other areas of the field. The terrain surrounding Spring Hill at the time was rolling, partially forested countryside dotted with farms and homesteads. Hood could not simply look through his field glasses to see progress in other areas, and he depended on mounted couriers for communication. Civil War campaigns and battles had, in varying degrees, such difficulties in common. The multitude of problems combining to cause disaster in middle Tennessee can be most closely encompassed within a single word: communication. Though lack of tangible evidence and mystery surround many of Spring Hill's key events, communication among Hood, Cheatham, Forrest, and others emerges as the significant complication.

Historians McWhiney and Jamieson have illustrated in great detail the cost of aggressive tactics characteristic of the Confederacy. The disintegration of the officer corps in the Southern armies is most telling, and during the hectic hours around Spring Hill, this fact loomed large. One can, for example, speculate about how things would have turned out if Hood and Hardee had been more compatible and if Cheatham had remained a divisional commander. The losses of aggressive and competent Major General H. T. Walker at Atlanta, and Lieutenant General Leonidas Polk, who fell at Pine Mountain, are prominent examples of damage to the Tennessee army's infrastructure.

The high pressure situation at Spring Hill demanded experienced personnel. From the moment the infantry came onto the field, at around 3:00 p.m., more than one general issued conflicting orders. Unintentionally, Hood and Cheatham competed against one another. When Hood countermanded Cheatham's order to General Bate to support Cleburne's left, for instance, one wonders whether anyone attempted to inform Cheatham of the change. His subsequent behavior indicates that he remained unaware. Perhaps a messenger detailed to tell him of the change failed to get it done. Whatever the cause, it constituted a serious breakdown in command structure.

In two cases, failure to communicate caused a heartbreaking amount of trouble. The stalled attack in which Cleburne had initially experienced success but lacked the power to overwhelm the enemy because of Bate's absence, and Bate being pulled away from the pike at a critical time stands as keys to Hood's failure to isolate and destroy Schofield's army at Spring Hill. In short, when Hood removed Bate's division from the force attacking Stanley in order to use it to block the pike and sweep toward Columbia, Cheatham should have been immediately informed. Cheatham, for his part, should have chosen other troops to replace those of Bate. After all, A. P. Stewart's corps was nearby at the time. In any case, Bate's initial refusal to obey and his statement that General Hood had ordered him to where he was should have been enough for Cheatham to figure things out. The fact that he failed to do so says much about his ability to command such large numbers in a situation that demanded quick decision making.

Brown's problem with the "phantom troops" supposedly overlapping his right could be termed "bad luck," and because of this information, Cheatham swayed Hood into believing that Stewart's corps was needed to support Brown's division. Both generals had a poor sense of where their lines actually were at the time. Two mitigating factors, unfamiliarity with the ground and rapidly approaching darkness, however, account for some of the confusion.

Both Hood and Cheatham suffered from inexperience in the roles they filled during the Tennessee campaign. Both men had acquired substantially more responsibility after Atlanta, but even so, they had only about ten weeks to adjust to their new situation. Certainly, as head of the army, Hood deserved blame for not taking a greater supervisory role. Like his mentor, General Lee, he left too much to his subordinates. For Lee, this practice proved most costly at Gettysburg; for Hood, it would be at Spring Hill. Hood's second-in-command, Cheatham, moved large bodies of men around on the battlefield that afternoon, and four occasions merit particular attention. First, he halted Cleburne's attack while he searched for General Brown. Second, he stopped action again because of phantom troops reported by General Strahl; and third, he pulled Bate back from seizing the pike. Finally, he convinced Hood to direct Stewart's corps to support Brown and mistakenly assured his commanding general that Stewart's men would also cover the road. Each of these variables added together point to the disaster at Franklin as the end result. A single variable removed may well have prevented the following day's tragedy.

Stress and the fast-moving pace of events caused General Cheatham to lose sight of the big picture, and Hood's physical condition may have detracted from his performance, making it harder for him to physically oversee fast-developing events on the battlefield. Extreme fatigue influenced the performance of private soldiers and officers alike. Exhaustion caused General Govan's men to lie down on the field during the stalled attack. Hood's men marched over two hundred miles after leaving their camps at Palmetto on September 29 before reaching their crossing point on the Tennessee River at Florence, Alabama. The Army of Tennessee's soldiers moved on meager rations, and while Sherman remained in the hunt, troops benefited little from sleep.

As previously noted, historian Clifford Dowdy described Hood as a natural fighter, a man who knew instinctively what should be done on the battlefield. Indeed, Hood's conduct at Eltham's Landing, Gaines Mill, Antietam, Second Manassas, and Gettysburg bear this estimation out. His quick decisions after crossing Rutherford's Creek to seize the Columbia Pike and attack Stanley's division stationed around Spring Hill also demonstrate his competence. His fighting instinct put him in company with Robert E. Lee, Stonewall Jackson, and Forrest. Hood's orders on the afternoon on November 29 were clear, but his failure lay in following Lee's example and trusting subordinates to carry them out.

Fifteen-year-old Hardin Figuers, who lived on the Main Street in Franklin, remembered that "about sun up [the Federal army] began pouring into town."[234] Tennessee historian Eric Jacobson writes, "Exhausted, hungry, and cold, the blue-clad troops stumbled toward Franklin, shaking their heads at how they had managed to slip past the enemy." General Hood remarked that Union soldiers marched "along the road almost under the light of the campfires of the main body of . . . [our] army." The retreat had not been orderly, however, and a feeling of suppressed panic filled the hearts of many, especially for the last units to pass through rebel lines: "I was on picket duty the night of Nov. 29," an Illinois soldier remembered, "just at daybreak, I saw a new regiment breaking camp in a hurry . . . . They skedaddled and left their new tents, knapsacks, guns, and cartridge boxes scattered around."[235]

Upon reaching Franklin, Union soldiers immediately began to strengthen defensive works that had existed around the town since its first occupation by United States troops in 1863. Lieutenant William Mohrmann of the 72nd Illinois wrote that "we arrived . . . hungry and tired out, half dead with want of sleep. We drew rations, made coffee, were given an allowance of whiskey—ominous sign—and set to fortify."[236] Fannie Courtney, 19, whose home stood near the town square, stated that 'the retreating army arrived . . . tired and many almost exhausted.' They commenced immediately throwing up breastworks. You would have been astonished

[234] David R. Logsdon, ed., *Eyewitnesses at the Battle of Franklin* (Nashville: Kettle Mills Press, 2000), 13.

[235] Gillum, *The Battle of Spring Hill*, 205-206; Jacobson, *For Cause and Country*, 178; Hood, *Advance and Retreat*, 287-288.

[236] Logsdon, ed., *Eyewitnesses at the Battle of Franklin*, 2.

to see how quick the work was completed and with what strength."[237] Preparations included chopping down a fruit orchard, a locust grove, and an orange hedge on the property of Fountain Branch Carter which lay at what would later become the battle's epicenter. Eight-year-old Alice McPhail Nichol, who lived in the Carter home, remembered "how frightened I was when they told us children to keep in the house, for the Yankees were coming; then I was told that the Rebels were coming to drive the Yankees out of town and how relieved we children were. We were afraid of the very name of Yankee."[238]

Soldiers used the wood from the orchard as part of an abatis before the line. Schofield had planks laid across the railroad bridge which had been partially damaged and detailed engineers to rebuild another one that had been burnt. A continuous line of defensive works, anchored at both ends of the full and rapidly flowing Harpeth River, defended the Union position. As soon as possible, Schofield began moving wagons across the rail bridge to facilitate his retreat.

At Spring Hill, feelings of disbelief and anger quickly spread among officers and men. That morning, John Copley of the 49th Tennessee, along with two other men and a sergeant, stood in awe of General Forrest's display of frustration: "[He] was so enraged that his face turned almost to a chalky whiteness . . . . He cursed out some of the commanding officers . . . for allowing the Federal Army to escape. I looked at him as he sat in his saddle pouring forth his volumes of wrath."[239] General Hood at breakfast that morning displayed similar feelings. Jacobson writes that "Hood wasted little time making his disappointment and anger evident at the 'unseemly affair.' He [fumed] about what had happened or not happened . . . and Cheatham took the brunt of [his] anger."[240] One officer present described him as "Wrathy as a rattlesnake." Mrs. Nathaniel Chears, in whose home the breakfast took place, stated that "language tossed about that morning was not fit for a woman's ears."[241] Hood lost little time in getting his army into marching order and in pursuit of Schofield.

During the march held at quick time, Confederate soldiers witnessed evidence that the Yankees had fled in disorderly panic. One soldier wrote, "We counted thirty-four wagons which were burned . . . . In some instances, whole teams of mules [had been] killed without being taken from the wagons."[242] Such sights heartened some but angered others. Chaplain McNeilly of Quarles's Brigade saw Forrest sitting on his horse at the side of the road looking at the evidence of hasty retreat and approached him. "He seemed to be in a rage," McNeilly recalled. "As I looked at his splendid physique and noticed his intense excitement, he seemed to me the most

---

[237]   Ibid.

[238]   Ibid.

[239]   Gillum, *The Battle of Spring Hill*, 209.

[240]   Jacobson, *For Cause and Country*, 202.

[241]   Ibid., footnote 16, p. 203.

[242]   John Simpson, ed., *Reminiscences of the 41ˢᵗ Tennessee*, 96.

THOMAS J. BROWN

76

dangerous animal I ever saw."[243] McNeilly's comments about Forrest say much about the man himself but also reveal much about the condition of Hood's army.

At 2:30 p.m., Hood held a council of war at the Harrison House where Cheatham, Cleburne, and Forrest advised against making a direct assault. Forrest wanted to flank the Union position. Though his idea held interesting possibilities, it also contained serious practical difficulties. He requested the loan of two thousand infantry and proposed crossing the Harpeth at one of the few fords below the town. He would then travel east of the Union lines and arrive at a place known as "Hollow Tree" or "Holly Tree" gap. From there, he could emerge north of Franklin and block the route to Nashville.[244]

Forrest could not have traveled by a direct route, and to avoid Wilson's cavalry and artillery placed on that side of the river, he needed to loop further East. The total distance was approximately fifteen miles. If Forrest had been ready to march when he proposed the plan, at 2:30 p.m., he would have had only two hours of daylight remaining. Lack of readiness would have caused significant delay, and that, combined with marching through unfamiliar territory, presented time-consuming difficulties. In the end, Forrest probably would not have arrived at Hollow Tree Gap before 10:00 p.m. By that time, Schofield's army could have been across the river on repaired bridges and, with the advantage of one of the few macadamized roads, been well on its way to Nashville before Forrest could put his flanking move into effect. Potentially, it could have been an ironic repetition of the fiasco at Spring Hill.[245]

Forrest must have been aware of potential problems with his plan, and it is surprising that he expressed such confidence in proposing it to Hood. He declared that he could complete the flanking move within two hours, which seems wildly optimistic. Cavalry alone might have done this, but two thousand tired infantrymen would not have been able to keep up. Perhaps Forrest felt guilty about troops under his command failing to block the road the previous night which would have been a far better time to offer to take action with the aid of two thousand infantry. Perhaps

---

[243]   Gillum, *The Battle of Spring Hill*, 211.

[244]   www.jbhhs.com, website for the John Bell Hood Historical Society. Here I found the most thorough discussion of Forrest's plan. Title page "Nashville: The 1864 Tennessee Campaign." While in Tennessee in April of 2006, I was able to view Forrest's proposed route from Winstead Hill. Not only would he have been in plain view from Fort Granger, Schoflield's headquarters during the battle, but also would have had to contend with Wilson's cavalry corps lurking in the area.

[245]   www.jbhhs.com, id.; In the mid-1830s British engineers John Metcalf and J. L. MacAdam "built roads that were well ballasted, surfaced and drained and as a result . . . the journey time between . . . towns and cities was sharply reduced." A road built and surfaced in this way was said to have been macadamized. Donald Cardwell, *The Norton History of Technology* (New York, London: W. W. Norton Company, 1994), 225.

some of the "volumes of wrath" poured forth that morning may have been directed at himself.[246]

At the time, the generals met, as the bulk of Hood's army rapidly approached Franklin, the United States troops stationed on hills around the town began to melt away, retreating behind the safety of their own fortifications. Hood, standing on Winstead Hill at the time, had a clear view of where the battle would be fought. In the distance, the line of Union works could be seen along with movement of wagons across the Harpeth. Sergeant Major Cunningham remarked that "the enemy was greatly excited. We could see them running to and fro."[247]

Wiley Sword, Thomas Connelly, and James McDonough have asserted that Hood's rage over the debacle at Spring Hill determined his decision to charge the Union works at Franklin, but observations of Hood at the time are contradictory. Sergeant Major Cunningham noted Hood's calm demeanor: "General Hood rode up to our lines, having his escort and staff in the rear . . . He remained at the front in plain view of the enemy for, perhaps, half an hour making a most careful study of their lines."[248] Hood had been clearly and understandably angry in the morning. His orders had not been carried out, communication had broken down, and most galling of all, Schofield's army had simply walked out of his trap. By the afternoon, anger had likely been replaced with grim determination to make good his final opportunity.

General George Thomas contacted Schofield prior to the battle, informing him that A. J. Smith's men had finally arrived, minus a division. Thomas wondered whether the position at Franklin could be held for three days while the rest of Smith's force came up. At 3:00 p.m., however, Schofield answered that he did not think it possible to hold on for more than a day, saying: "A worse position than this for an inferior force could hardly be found."[249] Despite his misgivings, Schofield did not think Hood would attack his fortified lines; instead, he feared a crossing of the river.

Hood's attack went forward at 4:00 p.m., and some noted a strange stillness prior to the advance. A surgeon with the 22nd Mississippi commented that "while the troops [took] their . . . positions, General Hood, with his staff, rode to the crest of [Winstead] hill, near where Dr. Wall and I [sat]. I remarked to the doctor: 'How strange the enemy do not open on us with their cannon! I do not like this quietness. It is ominous.'"[250] John M. Copley of the 49th Tennessee likened the silence to "one

---

[246]   Ibid.

[247]   Simpson, ed., *Reminiscences of the 41st Tennessee,* 97.

[248]   Ibid.

[249]   OR: I: XLV: I, 1171.

[250]   Logsdon, ed. *Eyewitnesses at the Battle of Franklin,* 13. Union artillery wisely held fire. The two mile range outdistanced effectiveness. (See my discussion of Hood not waiting for S. D. Lee's artillery to arrive, pages 79-80).

of those sickening lulls which [precede] a tremendous thunderstorm."[251] Hood's army consisted of three corps, but that of S. D. Lee being absent, he went forward only with those of Cheatham and Stewart. Hood aimed at breaking the Union center with the concentrated force of these two units. Cheatham's old division and that of Pat Cleburne judged Hood's most veteran, and hardest hitting troops would strike the Union troops stationed near the Carter House with overwhelming force.

Union General Wagner foolishly placed his division in advance of the main line. In effect, he created a salient much as Sickles had done at Gettysburg. Perhaps Wagner entertained dreams of glory, felt convinced that Hood would never attack or as General David Stanley later claimed, "was full of whiskey."[252] Whatever the cause, his men would not hold their place on the field for long.

The attack moved forward with impressive élan. Lieutenant Edwin Reynolds of the 50th Tennessee remembered that as the "long lines of infantry moved steadily and grandly through the open fields . . . the band of the fifth struck up 'Dixie,' and for once and only once, we went into battle cheered by . . . martial music."[253] The sight of Hood's relentlessly advancing columns greatly impressed Yankees waiting behind their breastworks. One declared it to be "worth a year of one's lifetime to witness the marshaling and advance of the rebel line of battle. Emerging from the woods in the most perfect order, nothing could be more suggestive of strength and discipline and restless power than was this long line of gray advancing over the plain."[254] Union Lieutenant Ambrose Bierce, later to become famous for his prose, described the confederates as "an unending column of gray and steel."[255] The coming attack caused great consternation in the ranks of Wagner's men: "The indignation of the men grew almost to a mutiny. The swearing of those gifted in profanity exceeded all their previous efforts," and many openly questioned the sanity of their officers.[256] Wagner stubbornly held his troops in line until the pressure became too great to bear. As rebel troops approached, threatening to simply gobble them up, the Yankees cracked under the strain and fled in wild panic for the safety of their lines. Captain Shellenberger of the 64th Ohio described how the break started: "It ran along our line so rapidly that it reminded me of a train of powder burning."[257] This footrace to the breastworks opened up an opportunity for the Confederates because Union troops behind the works hesitated to fire at the enemy for fear of hitting their comrades.

---

[251]   Ibid.

[252]   Jacobson, *For Cause and Country.* 284.

[253]   Logsdon ed., *Eyewitnesses at the Battle of Franklin,* 17.

[254]   McMurry, *John Bell Hood,* 175.

[255]   William McCann, ed., *Ambrose Bierce's Civil War,* "What Occurred at Franklin "(New York: Wing's Books, 1956), 67-69.

[256]   Logsdon ed., *Eyewitnesses at the Battle of Franklin,* 16.

[257]   Ibid., 22.

Confusion reigned as a mixture of Cleburne and Wagner's men burst through the Union center, the point where the Columbia Pike entered Franklin. One soldier remarked that Hood's men "swept on like a restless flood, coming in through our front line . . . . After passing through, they swept down in our rear carrying everything before them."[258] A serious breach developed and disaster threatened. The "gray masses converged into the gap, pushed through and then spreading, turned our men out of their works so hardly held against the attack in their front," wrote Bierce, stationed with other officers on a bluff across the river. "From our position . . . we could mark the constant widening of the gap, the steady encroachment of that blazing and smoking mass against its discarded opposition."[259]

Fortunately for Schofield, Colonel Emerson Opdyke's brigade, which contained the 125th Ohio, "Opdyke's Tigers" of Chickamauga fame, had positioned itself a short distance behind where the breakthrough occurred. Opdyke had originally been sent further back, but he ignored Wagner's orders, refusing further movement until his men could eat and rest. For this reason, the brigade stood ready to save the fortunes of the army. In a short but intensely violent mêlée, involving hand-to-hand fighting with clubbed muskets and bayonets, Opdyke's men managed to plug the gap, and the greatest single chance for Confederate success ground to a halt. Here, Hood's gamble died.

Hood intended that the divisions heading the attack would arrive together and hit the enemy position with concentrated force, but he failed to recognize the poor physical condition of his troops. The Confederate juggernaut lost cohesion: not because of irregularities in the field, but because of fatigue. Lieutenant Reynolds of the 5th Tennessee remarked that "our lines had become broken, and men rushed forward regardless of order . . . ."[260] Hood's army had been in almost constant motion ever since crossing the Tennessee. Its last time of significant rest had been at Florence, Alabama, while awaiting supplies. Harsh weather and scant rations had taken their toll. Men arrived on the field before Franklin exhausted by a seven-mile march carried out at quick time. Confederate Sam Watkins wrote that the "army had been depleted of its strength by a forced march from Spring Hill, and [that] stragglers lined the road."[261] Lieutenant Reynolds stated that many men, upon reaching the Union works, "fell down exhausted and out of breath."[262] A Union officer recalled seeing rebel soldiers "so tired that they seemed scarcely able to put one foot before the other. Many . . . fell against the outside face of the parapet and

---

[258]   U.S. Lieutenant Thoburn, 50th Ohio, Strickland's Brigade, in Logsdon, *Eyewitnesses at the Battle of Franklin*, 29.

[259]   McCann, ed., *Ambrose Bierce's Civil War*, 67-69.

[260]   Logsdon ed., *Eyewitnesses at the Battle of Franklin*, 30.

[261]   Watkins, *Company Aytch*, 201.

[262]   Logsdon ed., *Eyewitnesses at the Battle of Franklin*, 30.

lay there, panting."[263] The forced march to Franklin combined with nearly two miles at "quick time" separated the weak from the strong. Hood's gamble in making the attack is understandable, but in forcing his men forward with little opportunity for recovery, he expected too much. His attack might have possessed greater force had his troops gone forward with the "common step" used by Lee at Gettysburg.[264]

When their attack lost impetus, Confederate troops found themselves pinned down within a small strip of space outside Union works. They faced a deadly conundrum; moving forward or back proved suicidal, yet they made over twelve charges at terrible sacrifice and without success. Stewart's corps on the right faced enfilading fire from Fort Granger across the river, and Union guns blasted holes in their ranks. The attack ground to a halt all down the line. Bierce noted that "all over the country in [the Confederate] rear, clear back to the base of the hills, drifted the wreck of the battle . . . ."[265]

As darkness settled over the field, screams and groans of the wounded and dying could be heard, and lanterns seen bobbing along as medical personnel attempted to recover as many men as possible. Sam Watkins remarked that "the death angel was there to gather its . . . harvest; it was the grand coronation of death."[266]

At 7:10 p.m., General Thomas received news of Hood's unsuccessful assault from Schofield. He also gave Thomas a fairly accurate estimate of Southern loss, between five and six thousand. Thomas expressed great satisfaction in his reply: "It is glorious news, and I congratulate you and the brave men of your command."[267] He went on, however, to warn Schofield that the rebel army, though badly wounded, remained dangerous, and he told him to retire to Nashville via Brentwood where General Steedman would meet him with five thousand men. In fact, total Confederate casualties numbered around 6,500, with 1,700 dead. This last figure included six generals who led their men into battle: Pat Cleburne, Hiram Granbury, States Rights Gist, John Adams, Otho Strahl, and John C. Carter. Some of their bodies would be laid out on the porch of the nearby Carnton Plantation house.

Unlike the harsh weather that preceded it, November 30, the day of the battle, had been unseasonably warm. Dawn on December 1, however, told a different story with cold temperatures and an overcast sky. The gray morning light revealed the dead "piled up like stacks of wheat or scattered about like sheaves of grain," and a thin layer of frost covered the still forms like a funeral pall.[268]

---

[263] Ibid., 27.

[264] Shelby Foote, *The Civil War-A Narrative-Fredericksburg to Meridian* (New York: Random House, 1963), 553. Foote defines the "common step" as "a steady rate of about one hundred yards a minute."

[265] McCann, ed., *Ambrose Bierce's Civil War*, 67-69.

[266] Watkins, *Company Aytch*, 201.

[267] OR: I: XLV: I, 1171.

[268] Jacobson, F*or Cause and Country*, 431. (The agricultural imagery is General Cheatham's.)

General Hood and part of his staff rode into town amid an eerie silence. One soldier remembered how "Hood stopped close to where I was standing and took a long . . . view of the arena of the awful contest . . . His sturdy visage assumed a melancholy appearance, and for a considerable time, he sat on his horse and wept like a child."[269] Exhausted and emotionally overwrought, he noticed a chair in someone's front yard, had one of the men help him off his horse, and sat down. Hunched into his great coat, his hat low on his head, he stared out into the haunted landscape.[270]

McMurry notes that speculations by historians about Hood's behavior at Franklin have centered on three themes. First, Hood has been portrayed as an insensitive fiend, a man "crazed by pain and frustration who 'reveled in blood.'" This character sent his men into the inferno at Franklin in order to discipline them for previous failures. Second, is the theory that Hood became infected with his army's desire for revenge over failures at Spring Hill and became convinced that his soldiers could successfully assault the Union lines at Franklin. Finally, it has been suggested that Hood somehow reverted mentally to 1862, remembering the costly success of Gaines Mill. All of these are, as McMurry writes, speculation, and there is no way that we can ever know exactly what thoughts went through Hood's mind as his men readied themselves for battle.[271]

Practicalities also overrule such historical ruminations. From the moment his army crossed into Tennessee, it had been Hood's goal to destroy Schofield's force before it could unite with Thomas at Nashville. Jacobson remarks that it is simplistic to characterize Hood as a general whose tactical thinking limited itself to the frontal assault, and McMurry comments that he was not "the boneheaded simpleton that many writers have depicted."[272] At Gettysburg, Hood argued against attacking through Devil's Den and instead advocated moving around Little Round Top where Confederates could come in behind the Union troops. At Atlanta, he fought "four major battles . . . . One of them involved a significant flanking maneuver and another developed into a series of wasted frontal assaults due more . . . to errors by S. D. Lee than anything Hood did."[273] He attempted to flank Schofield first at Columbia and

[269]   Ibid., 437; Logsdon, *Eyewitnesses at the Battle of Franklin,* 83-84, the quotation came from a Confederate artillery man named Bowers.

[270]   Logsdon ed., *Eyewitness at the Battle of Franklin,* Alice McPhail Nichol, eight years old at the time, "saw a man sitting in a chair in the yard. He looked so sad, and grandpa told me that was Gen. Hood." 84.

[271]   McMurry, *John Bell Hood,* 174-175.

[272]   Ibid., 191.

[273]   Jacobson, *For Cause and Country,* 253. Also see Russell S. Bonds, *War Like the ThunderBolt: The Battle and Burning of Atlanta* (Yardley, Pennsylvania: Westholme Publishing, LLC, 2009), Chapters 4, 5, 6, 7, 9. These include the battles of Peachtree Creek, Bald Hill or the Battle of Atlanta, Ezra Church, and Jonesboro.

then at Spring Hill. As has been noted above, a variety of logistical and personnel problems prevented success, and all the while, Schofield drew closer to Nashville. By the time the Union army reached Franklin, it stood only fifteen miles from its goal. Hood is almost universally criticized for not awaiting S. D. Lee's corps and the bulk of his artillery to arrive. It is thought that bombardment may have broken up Schofield's defenses. Three problems loomed large: daylight, which was essential for accurate artillery fire; distance; and fatigue. Nearly two miles of open ground lay between Hood's assembly point at Winstead Hill and the Union line at Franklin, too far for effective artillery. Six and twelve pounder field guns, most common in both armies, had a maximum range of 1,523 yards or not quite a mile with their barrels raised to maximum elevation. Rifled guns, not as plentiful, possessed greater potential; a three-inch gun, for example, had a maximum range of 3,110 yards, using ordinary powder, still not quite the two-mile distance between Hood's lines and those of the enemy.[274]

In order to achieve maximum effect, Hood would not only have had to wait for S. D. Lee's corps to arrive but would then have had to haul the guns over a mile closer to Franklin. Lee's corps would not have arrived until well after sundown, and emplacing the guns would have taken several hours. In all likelihood, the artillery would not have been ready until sometime the following morning at which point Schofield's army would have decamped and been well on their way to Nashville. Hood knew this based upon the Union general's previous behavior. Waiting for the next morning, in Hood' mind, presented an even bigger gamble than making the attack at 4:00 p.m. He counted upon being able to hit the Union center with Cheatham's battle-hardened corps hard enough to crack it before full darkness came on. He hoped for the effect of a lightning strike. At Gaines Mill, Hood had seen how such an assault could be successful; he knew the risks and chose to take them.[275]

---

[274] John Gibbon, *The Artillerist's Manual* (Dayton, Ohio: Morningside, 1991) 455. This is a facsimile of the original published in 1860 as a text to be used by West Point cadets.

[275] Groom, *Shrouds of Glory*, 217-218. Provides a concise discussion of Franklin's "what-ifs, might have dones, could have dones, [and] should have dones."

CHAPTER 4

Nashville

In Franklin's aftermath, Hood had several alternatives to ponder. More considerations presented themselves than simply marching on to Nashville. His opposite number, Union General George H. Thomas, also faced significant problems that needed solving in the face of Hood's approach. For the Southern commander, a rapidly decaying Confederacy would prove unable to supply him with desperately needed reinforcements and equipment. Thomas, on the other hand, would receive what he required but only days before battle. How the two men dealt with such challenges and the ultimate result will be the focus of this chapter.

Hood's first choice could be to admit failure of the campaign and retreat into Alabama, there to refit and prepare to fight another day. Alternatively, the Army of Tennessee could march on Murfreesboro, possibly defeat the Union garrison there, and "reestablish the status quo of 1862." The third option involved marching around Nashville, crossing the Cumberland River, and attacking Union communications. In theory, this would force Thomas to fight outside of Nashville's fortifications and on ground of Hood's choosing. The fourth choice, advancing quickly upon the Tennessee capital and assaulting enemy lines, Hood quickly rejected as suicidal given the damage already sustained at Franklin. Instead, he settled upon forming a defensive perimeter in the hills just outside Nashville while improving his own supply lines and sending for reinforcements from the Trans Mississippi.[276]

Hood rejected any retrograde movement unless made in order to form a juncture with reinforcements and that only, as he explained, "with the avowed intention to march back again upon Nashville."[277] Echoing Frederick the Great and Napoleon, who believed that desertion could be controlled by keeping men active during difficult times, Hood declared "it more judicious . . . that [his army] should face decisive issue rather than retreat" and further that his men could not march away without having made a final "vigorous effort . . . to save the [Confederacy]

---

[276] Stanley F. Horn, *The Decisive Battle of Nashville* (Baton Rouge: LSU Press, 1956, 1984), 21.

[277] Hood, *Advance and Retreat*, 299.

from disaster."[278] Such comments reflect prevailing aggressive and regionally defensive attitudes common among the military and political ruling classes in the South as detailed by historians Grady McWhiney and Perry Jamieson in *Attack and Die,* but they also conceal fear of retreating with an already weakened army, while high numbers of war weary men simply left the ranks and headed homeward. Hood failed to mention desertion as a significant problem, except for scattered references to "stragglers" in wartime correspondence or his memoirs. In the latter case, Hood may have been concerned about insulting the honor of former soldiers and the prevailing influence of Lost Cause propaganda which sought not only to romanticize the Confederacy but also sought to find scapegoats and excuses rather than facing hard reasons for defeat.

Historian Mark Weitz reveals that desertion emerged as a serious problem as early as 1862, and it grew worse as Southern fortunes plummeted. He states that soldiers felt most justification to leave the army while stationed in or passing through their home states. Redeployment and retreat provided additional motivation as men felt threatened moving further away from home or began to see the war effort as hopeless. According to Weitz, desertion increased within the Army of Tennessee from the fall of Atlanta when it marched away from Georgia, spent three weeks waiting for supplies in Alabama, and then crossed into Tennessee.[279] Undoubtedly, the specter of desertion influenced Hood's decisions. Colonel George William Brent remarked in General Orders number six issued on December 7 that "General Beauregard has seen, with pain and mortification, that large numbers of the Confederate cavalry are absent from their colors without leave, avoiding all duty . . . [and] roaming over the country engaged in the pillage and robbery of defenseless women and loyal citizens . . . devastating a fair and fruitful country on the productions of which our country depends."[280]

The presence of Union General Lovell Rousseau's force of "eight thousand men heavily entrenched"[281] made the idea of marching on Murfreesboro problematic. The town was situated about twenty-five miles from Nashville, and if Hood could not subdue the blue troops quickly, it would not be difficult for Thomas to march to their aid. The Confederates would thus find themselves caught between two forces. Additionally, Rousseau could further reinforce Thomas's already superior army or attack Hood once he became engaged at Nashville. In short, Rousseau's garrison acted both as a threat and as a distraction. Hood could not afford to ignore Rousseau, but he wanted to nullify the menace with as little loss to himself as possible. By December 7, the situation became more tense when a message from Beauregard

---

[278]   Ibid.

[279]   Mark A. Weitz, *More Damning than Slaughter: Desertion in the Confederate Army* (Lincoln: University of Nebraska Press, 2005), 254-255.

[280]   OR: I: XLV: II, 658.

[281]   Hood, *Advance and Retreat,* 300.

informed Hood that fifteen thousand more Union troops had passed through Memphis en route to join Thomas.[282] General Forrest, supported by Bate's division and two additional brigades under Sears and Brown, had been detailed to contain Rousseau. A message sent to Forrest instructed him to "drive the enemy back [but not] to attack the enemy works."[283] News of Union reinforcements prompted Hood to order Bate's return to the army then forming in front of the Tennessee capital. Hood is criticized by historians for not keeping Forrest's cavalry at hand, but some check had to be exerted on Rousseau.

The other option of passing around Nashville, crossing the Cumberland River, and threatening Thomas's communications in order to lure him out of Nashville's fortifications, though plausible on the surface, faced several significant complications. Hood, no longer at full strength, could not risk being attacked by Thomas's now superior force while on the move. Crossing the Cumberland, engorged with water from almost continual rains, would have been sharply contested. Hood viewed the situation realistically, stating that "I could not venture with my small force to cross the Cumberland into Kentucky, without first receiving reinforcements from the Trans-Mississippi Department." He felt convinced that "Tennesseans and Kentuckians would not join our forces [if] we had failed . . . to defeat the Federal Army and capture Nashville."[284] Furthermore, Hood states that at this point, his men stood "sorely in need of shoes and clothing."[285]

Hood commented that prior to the Battle of Nashville, he possessed "an effective force of only twenty-three thousand and fifty three" and added that a Confederate spy network kept him well informed about Thomas's growing strength.[286] Harsh reality forced him to conclude that without reinforcements, "I was well aware of our inability to attack the Federals in their . . . stronghold with any hope of success."[287] Lacking significant reinforcements, the Southern commander found his choices limited.

For Hood, establishing fortified lines in front of Nashville and awaiting reinforcements or attack "which handsomely repulsed might afford . . . an opportunity to follow up our advantage . . . and enter the city on the heels of the enemy" seemed the best option under the circumstances.[288] To modern eyes, such thinking appears fatalistic and founded upon a false premise that Thomas might commit a major

---

[282]   OR: I: XLV: II, 640.

[283]   Ibid., 666. Colonel A. P. Mason, Hood's Assistant Adjutant General to Forrest.

[284]   Hood, *Advance and Retreat,* 299.

[285]   Ibid., 301. A communication to Colonel George Brent, Assistant Adjutant General at Montgomery, Alabama regarding supplies for Hood's army calls for "at least three thousand suits . . . together with the same number of pairs of shoes." Also see OR: I: XLV: II, 656.

[286]   Ibid., 299.

[287]   Ibid.

[288]   Ibid.

blunder. Hood, who first met the Union commander when a student at West Point in the early 1850s, should have known better. Thomas's careful preparation and attention to detail distinguished him from many other generals. This said, however, one of Hood's main goals had been to keep Thomas from getting up to full strength by capturing or destroying Schofield's army. In short, he had hoped to defeat Thomas in detail. This had not happened, and the closer Hood got to Nashville, the more desperate his situation became. Historical hindsight shows that if Hood was going to withdraw, he should have done so immediately following Franklin. Historians from Horn in the 1940s, Connelly in the 1960s, Sword in 1992, and, finally, Jacobson in 2006 have soundly condemned Hood for marching on Nashville after suffering significant losses along the Harpeth. The key question, however, lies in *when* Hood became fully informed of Thomas's strength. As previously noted, Hood commented in *Advance and Retreat* that he had been regularly given information by spies, but he did not indicate *when* this information began to emerge. Union generals—such as Grant, Sherman, and Thomas—knew about Confederate spies and took measures to limit their effectiveness. Cavalry patrols roamed the countryside looking for suspicious persons. In addition, communications within the *Official Records* reveal significant reinforcement to the Union army only *after* Franklin. That historians such as Horn, Sword, and McDonough have failed to enlarge upon this information is mysterious. Possibly, it indicates a too great reliance upon Lost Cause—approved sources within the *Southern Historical Society Papers* which seek mainly to condemn Hood and not to find reasonable explanations for his behavior prior to the Battle of Nashville.

Evidence provided by historian Thomas Van Horne and Colonel Henry Stone indicates strongly that it would have been impossible for Hood to know the full extent of Thomas's strength until after December 1. Stone comments that by that date, the Union army existed only as a composite force, "an ill-assorted and heterogeneous mass, not yet welded into an army."[289] Van Horne agrees, remarking that General Steedman's arrival from Chattanooga with five thousand men organized into a provisional division on the evening of December 1 represented the final addition to a diverse "improvised army [containing] three corps, each of which represented a distinct department . . . an infusion of raw infantry regiments; the greater portion of cavalry of the Military division of the Mississippi but still largely dismounted; and [black] soldiers who [would] have their first opportunity . . . to fight by brigades."[290] In short, though the army was coalescing, Thomas faced a formidable organizational task. Put simply, the situation resembled having all the parts of a powerful but disassembled engine lying on a shop floor.

[289]   Col. Henry Stone, "Repelling Hood's Invasion of Tennessee," in *Battles and Leaders of the Civil War*, Vol. IV (New York: The Century Co., 1884, 1888), 454.

[290]   Van Horne, *History of the Army of the Cumberland*, Volume II, 223.

Hood moved quickly after Franklin, setting up most of his lines near the Tennessee capital by December 3. The message regarding Union General Steele's force of fifteen thousand moving up from Memphis sent by Beauregard to Hood, for example, is dated December 2. Thomas's army accumulated most of its strength within the first two weeks of December, and Wilson's cavalry, upon which Thomas placed great importance, did not achieve full power until after December 7. In short, Hood determined not "to abandon the ground as long as [he] saw a shadow of assistance from the Trans-Mississippi Department or of victory in battle."[291] Thus, Hood could not have been fully informed until after the first week of December.

It is important to note that at this apparently hopeless juncture not one of Hood's superiors, from Confederate president Jefferson Davis to General Beauregard, recommended that he pull his army out of middle Tennessee. On the contrary, communications within the *Official Records* show these leaders doing all they could to improve Hood's supply line and to send him reinforcements. Hood is often assigned sole ownership of the Tennessee Campaign, but it did not belong to him alone. The Confederate high command gambled hugely when they committed themselves to the campaign.[292] Critical historians such as Connolly, McDonough, and Sword often write as if responsibility belonged solely to Hood, which in fact, it did not.

After December 3, Hood saw retreat as potentially more dangerous than awaiting attack. By remaining, his army could fight behind prepared positions. Had he attempted to pull back, Thomas would not have allowed him to escape. The Army of Tennessee would then have been caught in the open countryside while on the move. Brutally adverse weather and road conditions made movement extremely difficult. Hood's engineers would also have had to construct a pontoon bridge across the Tennessee River, high and fast from recent storms, while a superior enemy nipped at their heels. Though these circumstances eventually came to pass, Hood wanted to avoid them as long as some hope of success existed. In essence, after establishing its lines along the drenched and frozen hills outside of Nashville, the Tennessee army faced a deadly conundrum.

Across from Hood's position, his Union counterpart General George Thomas had been dealing with command and supply problems of his own. General Sherman, in preparing for the March to the Sea, dismantled Thomas's command, the Army of the Cumberland, in order to construct a powerful force for his invasion of Georgia. In doing so, he took the most accomplished officers and units. Thomas begged in vain that Sherman leave him the Fourteenth Corps as a basis from which to build a new army, but in the end, he was left with twenty thousand men, a mixture of

---

[291]   Hood, *Advance and Retreat*, 300.

[292]   OR: I: XLV: II, 639-40. Beauregard to General S. Cooper, Adjutant Inspector General, December 2. Beauregard to Gov. Joe Brown, December 2. Beauregard to General E. Kirby Smith, December 2.

green troops, veterans, and almost no cavalry. There were also many troops whose enlistment would soon expire. For Thomas, the dissolution of his former command must have been painful. He had been with this army from its infancy and played a major role in its construction beginning at Camp Dick Robinson, Kentucky, in 1861.[293] Thomas Buell argues that "Thomas made the Army of the Cumberland the most modern and lethal armed force of its day."[294] That Sherman needed such a powerful force to march through Georgia at a time when major Confederate armies camped elsewhere and Thomas faced Hood's battered but still dangerous veterans posed a significant question. Thomas, true to his professionalism, however, did not press the matter. Instead, he applied his considerable administrative skills to building a new force, one capable not only of defending Nashville but of achieving decisive victory. These efforts reached fruition only days before combat began.

Powerfully built at just under six feet and about 250 pounds, George Thomas shared Hood's Southern heritage. Born in Southampton County, Virginia, he grew up on a plantation worked by slaves. The significant difference between them lay in the fact that Thomas held the oath he had taken to the United States as sacred.[295] Moreover, Thomas possessed a smoldering conviction that Virginians had been tricked into secession by "hot-headed ambitious men chance and slavery had made leaders," and for him, "the Virginia ordinance of secession was a fraud."[296]

By 1861, Thomas had become one of the most experienced military officers in the United States. Graduating twelfth out of forty-two in the West Point class of 1840, he went on to serve with the 3rd artillery in the second Seminole War and later in Mexico as part of Zachary Taylor's army, fighting at Monterrey and Buena Vista. Following the treaty of Guadalupe Hidalgo, Thomas earned promotion to Captain. Historian Francis McKinney writes that "three brevet [promotions] in seven years marked [him] as one of the outstanding junior officers in the army."[297] Thomas served as instructor of artillery and cavalry tactics at West Point from 1851 to 1854 where cadet John Bell Hood attended his classes. In 1855, Thomas joined the elite 2nd Cavalry created by Secretary of War, Jefferson Davis, as major. There,

---

293   McKinney, Francis F., *Education in Violence: The Life of General George H. Thomas and the History of the Army of the Cumberland* (Chicago: Americana House Inc., 1991), Chapter 1, "Westward to Camp Dick Robinson," 113. McKinney notes that "before its first brigade was organized, Thomas was giving shape to that formidable military machine that was later to be the Army of the Cumberland."

294   Thomas B. Buell, *The Warrior Generals: Combat Leadership in the Civil War* (New York: Three Rivers Press, 1997), xxxi.

295   Frank A. Palumbo, *George Henry Thomas: The Dependable General* (Dayton, Ohio: Morningside House, Inc., 1983), 70.

296   Donn Piatt, *Major General George H. Thomas: Memoirs of Men Who Saved the Union* (New York: Belford Clarke Co., 1887), 81-82, in Palumbo, *George Henry Thomas*, 59.

297   McKinney, *Education in Violence*, 45.

Hood served as his aide-de-camp. Like many Union army officers, Thomas shared friendships with Southerners such as Robert E. Lee, Braxton Bragg, and William Hardee who would later battle for the Confederacy. When war broke out after the fall of Fort Sumter, Thomas served as colonel of the Second Cavalry and had developed expertise in artillery, cavalry, and infantry tactics.

In 1861, promoted to the rank of brigadier general and sent to the western theater, Thomas commanded elements of the army of Ohio. Troops under his direction scored the first Union victory in the West at Mill Springs, Kentucky, on January 19, 1862. Almost one year later, Thomas directed artillery that played a key role in achieving victory at Stones River, a battle that helped assure Union control of Middle Tennessee.[298] During the Tullahoma Campaign, June 22 to July 3, 1863, where the Army of the Cumberland then commanded by William Starke Rosecrans, brilliantly outmaneuvered Confederate General Bragg, Thomas had responsibility for its most important movement from Dechard to Chattanooga which resulted in a significant victory at Hoover's Gap.

On September 20, near a creek whose Indian name translates into "River of Death," Thomas earned his most famous sobriquet, "Rock of Chickamauga." Following a devastating Confederate breakthrough of the Union center, spearheaded by Longstreet's Corps and led by General Hood, Thomas rallied troops around him and retreated to high ground known as Horseshoe Ridge. With the rest of the army in disarray and rapidly retreating toward Chattanooga, he pulled together elements of scattered commands and held out until sunset, long enough to conduct an orderly withdrawal, saving the army from destruction. Not long after this achievement, Thomas was given charge of the army he had helped to create. At Missionary Ridge on November 25, during the battles of Chattanooga, Thomas's men dramatically stormed fortified positions on the high ground and secured victory for Grant. With his army forming the largest part of Sherman's combined force during the Atlanta campaign, Thomas served as second-in-command.

Thus, at Nashville, Hood faced a formidable adversary, a man who "understood and employed the combined arms of infantry, artillery, and cavalry as no other general on either side."[299] Southern heritage and army service were about all Hood and Thomas shared. The once dashing Confederate cavalier, whose physical injuries reflected the condition of his ragged army, fought to defend a dying culture. Thomas, solid and relentless, represented an industrialized modern nation moving toward the twentieth century.

Hood's army began building its defensive line on December 2 with the Confederates displaying, at least outwardly, great confidence. Historian Benson Bobrick writes that "bands [appeared] . . . trumpets blowing, drums beating, and

---

[298] James Lee McDonough, *Stones River: Bloody Winter in Tennessee* (Knoxville: University of Tennessee Press, 1980), 131.

[299] Bobrick, *Master of War*, xxxi.

strains of "Dixie" could be heard from a dozen or more points along the line."[300] Thomas, as yet unsure of enemy numbers and well aware of weaknesses in his army, telegraphed General Henry Halleck in Washington on December 1:

> After General Schofield's fight of yesterday, feeling convinced that the enemy very far outnumbered him . . . I determined to retire to the fortifications around Nashville until General Wilson can get his cavalry equipped. He has now but one fourth the number of the enemy and consequently is no match for him. I have two ironclads here with several gun boats, and commander Fitch assures me that Hood can neither cross the Cumberland nor blockade it . . . If Hood attacks me here, he will be more seriously damaged than he was yesterday. If he remains until Wilson gets equipped, I can whip him and will move against him at once. I have Murfreesboro strongly held and therefore feel easy in regard to its safety. Bridgeport, Stevenson, and Elk River bridges also have strong garrisons.[301]

Though Thomas expressed confidence in ultimate success and outlined the overall situation clearly, Halleck, Secretary of War Stanton, General-in-Chief Grant, and President Lincoln himself seem to have ignored the full meaning of his message. Instead, they saw in Thomas's desire to wait until Wilson's cavalry reached full readiness, just another excuse for delay.

On the morning of December 2, Stanton wired Grant that Lincoln felt "solicitous about the disposition of General Thomas to lay in fortifications for an indefinite period," adding somewhat hysterically that "this looks like the McClellan and Rosecrans strategy of do nothing and let the rebels raid the country."[302] Perhaps the Secretary of War exaggerated Lincoln's concern; much can be hidden behind a word like "solicitous," but we will never know the President's real thoughts.

General Grant then began a long, (and to Thomas) tiring series of hectoring messages, suggesting that Thomas arm Nashville's citizens to defend the city so that he could sally forth and attack Hood. Grant thus revealed a fundamental lack of knowledge about the political temper of the city's inhabitants, the majority of whom held pro-Confederate sentiments and had chafed under Union control since 1862. Thomas, having occupied the city for several months, understood the public mood. Grant further lectured that "instead of falling back to Nashville, we should have taken the offensive against the enemy" at Franklin.[303] Thomas replied that this was exactly what he had suggested but that "Schofield felt convinced that he could not hold the

---

[300]   Ibid., 276.

[301]   OR:I: XLV: II, 3.

[302]   OR: I: XLV: II, 15-16.

[303]   Ibid.

enemy at Franklin" until reinforcements arrived.[304] In ending a patient description of his situation, Thomas reminded Grant that "we can neither get reinforcements or equipment at this great distance from the North very easily" and furthermore that "it must be remembered that my command was made up of the two weakest corps of General Sherman's army and all the dismounted cavalry."[305] This last must have been difficult for Grant to digest. Though he had initially opposed Sherman's march to Savannah with such a large force while Hood remained on the field, he had nevertheless allowed himself to be talked into it. He was not alone; Lincoln, Stanton, and Halleck all shared in his responsibility and concerns.[306] Now, with a real crisis brewing in Tennessee, the decision had come back to haunt the Union high command. In addition to this, the Army of the Potomac (officially commanded by George Meade but really under Grant's control) had been bogged down in front of Lee's army at Petersburg since June.

The mood of the country weighed Grant down as newspaper articles expressed impatience, war weariness, and apprehension, if not outright fear, about what might happen at Nashville. Grant bought into public anxiety about Hood marching to the Ohio River or even as far as Chicago. We know now, with the aid of historical hindsight and Hood's own postwar comments, that he had no intention of moving further North or marching to the aid of General Lee without first taking Nashville. His army's crumbling supply line could not adequately deliver food, clothing, or equipment. Historian David Fraley remarks that at this point, the Army of Tennessee experienced some of the worst conditions of any army in history. Clad in rags, a high percentage of barefoot troops faced horrific weather conditions, while pickets froze to death during nights where the temperature hovered around zero.[307] To be fair, Grant did not have access to Hood's thoughts or full knowledge of his army's condition.

Despite outward displays of bravado, Confederate soldiers dug in along Hood's soggy, mist-shrouded lines and endured intense pain and hardship. Alabama soldier J. P. Cannon recorded December 11 as the coldest day he had ever experienced and wrote further about his "position in the open fields with [no shelter from] the force of the wind which is blowing a perfect gale from the north." Soldiers had "no wood to make fires and most of us thinly clad . . . . It seems like we are bound to freeze

---

[304]   Ibid.

[305]   OR: XLV: II, 17-18.

[306]   Bobrick, *Master of War*, 260, 261, 263.

[307]   David Fraley, former Carter House and Carnton Plantation curator, gave lectures on the battle of Nashville at a meeting of the John Bell Hood Historical Society that I attended in May of 2008. He commented that on the nights of December 11 and 12, the temperature was below zero.

unless a change occurs very soon."[308] Many found that the best way to reduce the effects of cold lay in burrowing like animals into the earth. Soldier George Brewer described how "men dug holes in the ground, constructing fireplaces in the earth on one side with barrel chimneys."[309] Another soldier added that "many more men would have died from exposure . . . had [it] not been for . . . getting under cover of the soil."[310] Warmer it may have been, but many noted the resemblance to "lying down in a soldier's grave."[311] Though better supplied with clothing, food, and fuel, Union soldiers also suffered. F. A. Cline of the 40th Missouri remarked that "it was all we could do to keep from freezing to death" and that "we have nothing to lie in but . . . small dog tents."[312]

Evidence of the war's corrosive effect upon society appeared throughout all areas of military operations. Confederate guerilla and deserter bands scoured the countryside in search of plunder, not only around Nashville but also in Kentucky. General S. S. Fry complained of "horrid outrages committed by a gang of guerillas," stating that "they have killed in a few days past some fourteen quiet, inoffensive citizens, among them one discharged soldier." Fry requested that he be allowed to use a 150-man detachment of Kentucky cavalry "to catch these scoundrels and afford [the] people (most of whom I know to be loyal) some relief."[313]

In taking advantage of his authorization from Stanton to appropriate mounts for the cavalry from wherever they could be found, General Wilson became, in the eyes of many citizens, ruthless. One Kentucky official wrote in outrage to the Secretary of War, "The general impressment of horses by the military is . . . oppressive . . . . All horses are taken without regard to the occupation of the owner or his loyalty. Loaded country wagons with produce for the market are left in the road; milk carts, drays, and butcher's wagons are left in the street, their horses seized."[314] Ironically, as armies are organizations that depend upon discipline and order to facilitate their function, their activities during wartime invariably inspire conditions of anarchy, official or otherwise.

For Thomas, equipping Wilson's cavalry held paramount importance because it would be used not only to help win the upcoming fight but also for the pursuit and as a tool to break up the enemy force. Thomas aimed at far more than winning a battle; he saw the destruction of Hood's army and elimination of Confederate resistance in the West to be of premier significance. Thus, attacking Hood before

---

[308]   James Lee McDonough, *Nashville: The Western Confederacy's Final Gamble* (Knoxville: University of Tennessee Press, 2004), 150.

[309]   Ibid.

[310]   Ibid.

[311]   Ibid.

[312]   Ibid., 151.

[313]   OR: I: XLV: II, 28.

[314]   Buell, *The Warrior Generals*, 399.

being fully prepared would not only result in unnecessary loss of life but also prevent him from finishing the job.

The contrast in tone between messages sent from Washington or Grant's headquarters at City Point and those from Nashville is notable. Military officers on the scene seem calm; they kept Hood under close observation and remained ready to react. For example, Colonel Hough, Thomas's assistant adjutant general, advised General McArthur, commanding the first division of the sixteenth corps, that "it is desirable that you have strong pickets in your post and your whole line in readiness to take arms at a moment's warning." Hough also stressed that "fires at the picket stations and on the tops of the hills must be discontinued entirely, and fires for cooking are only allowed in the main line which must be put out as soon as the cooking is done."[315] This order no doubt made life harder for soldiers already contending with the cold but showed Thomas standing prepared for any aggressive move.

By contrast, the tone of Grant's messages became increasingly nervous; the general-in-chief's fears that Hood would move northward increased with each passing day. On December 3, he commented acidly to Sherman that "Thomas has got back into the defenses of Nashville with Hood close upon him," making it sound as if the Confederates had Nashville under siege.[316] Thomas in fact busied himself making preparations to crush Hood. On the same day, he reported having "a good entrenched line on the hills around Nashville" and hoped "to be able to report ten thousand cavalry mounted and equipped in less than a week when I shall feel able to march against Hood."[317] Thomas's chief telegraph officer, Major J. C. Van Duzer, provided a good description of Union lines to Major Thomas T. Eckert, the government's head telegrapher in Washington along with an interesting remark about Forrest:

> Our earthworks reach from the Cumberland on the right to the Cumberland on the left, distant about two miles from capitol, average distance, forming nearly half circle, second line in weak places; it is a very strong line and strongly held . . . . Some skirmishing has occurred today, and upon a rebel column showing in the field . . . our artillery opened with shell and sent them to cover. Nothing heard of Forrest, but General Wilson is looking for him, and no apprehension is felt.[318]

General Thomas J. Wood, who had taken over command of the Fourth Corps for the injured Stanley, reported on December 3 that within a few more hours, his

---

[315]   OR: I: XLV: II, 22-23.

[316]   Ibid., 612.

[317]   OR: I: XLV: II, 22-23.

[318]   Ibid., 32.

line would be impregnable.[319] A circular went out that evening advising division commanders that reveille would occur at 4:30 a.m. the following morning, that "at earliest appearance of daylight . . . troops must be under arms."[320] From December 1 and right up to the first day of battle on the fifteenth, a stable but uneasy atmosphere existed between the two armies. Though ample communications between Thomas and Washington showed this to be true, the general-in-chief continued to press for immediate action. As Van Horne put it, "Delay for any cause [displeased] General Grant."[321]

After remaining quiet for a single day, Grant started badgering Thomas again on the fifth. He continued to worry about Forrest and remarked that "Hood should be attacked where he is. Time strengthens him, in all probability, as much as it does you."[322] This last revealed ignorance of the actual situation. General Grant, hundreds of miles away at City Point, concocted his opinions and fears in another world. Hood actually grew weaker as Thomas grew stronger. Buell comments that requests coming from the Army of Tennessee for clothing and reinforcements went largely unanswered. In many ways, Hood's situation reflected the disintegration of Confederate infrastructure as a whole.

Thomas, perhaps sensing the futility of reasoning with Grant, contacted Halleck two hours later, "I have been along my entire line today. The enemy has not advanced at all since the third instant." He further remarked upon a key Confederate weakness: "Prisoners we have taken . . . report that Hood has to draw . . . supplies from the Memphis and Charleston Railroad, wagoning from Cherokee Station."[323] In some ways, Hood's starved situation, depending upon a thin and vulnerable supply line, reflected that experience by Thomas at Chattanooga in 1863. For Hood, however, there would be no arrival of reinforcements or opening of a "cracker line."

Grant's patience continued to fray, and on the sixth, he wired Thomas demanding that he "attack Hood at once . . . wait no longer . . . [to] remount your cavalry. There is great danger of delay resulting in a campaign back to the Ohio River."[324] The next day, Stanton added fuel to Grant's fire. He too seemed panicky about Nashville, remarking that if Thomas waited for Wilson's cavalry to be fully equipped, "Gabriel will be blowing his last horn."[325] Grant replied by saying that if Thomas continued to delay, he should be replaced by Schofield.

On December 9, one of the worst storms in history struck middle Tennessee. Ironically, with both armies literally frozen in place, Grant chose this time to issue

---

[319]   Ibid., 33.

[320]   Ibid., Circular No. 22.

[321]   Van Horne, *The History of the Army of the Cumberland,* Volume II, 225.

[322]   OR: I: XLV: II, 55.

[323]   Ibid.

[324]   Ibid., 70.

[325]   OR: I: XLV: II, 84.

his first order, removing Thomas from command. Fortunately, General Halleck delayed passing it on, and after hearing of the storm's severity from Thomas, Grant backtracked.[326] In his next wire, he told Thomas that he seemed to be "slow" and in an earlier exchange remarked to Stanton that he saw Thomas as "too cautious to ever take the initiative."[327] Had Grant forgotten how quickly Thomas reacted after the Confederate breakthrough at Chickamauga? Indeed, had he forgotten that troops under Thomas's command had taken the initiative at Missionary Ridge and broken the back of rebel resistance? It seems Grant became the victim of stress-induced myopia. He saw only what he feared most, the specter of Hood's army marching toward the Ohio with a too slow Thomas in vain pursuit.

Thomas informed Grant on the ninth that "a terrible storm of freezing rain [had] been pouring down since daylight."[328] He had been aiming at attacking Hood on the 10th, but weather conditions overrode his desire. For five days rain, sleet and ice victimized Unionist and Confederate alike. Firewood became almost as important as food to such an extent that "the once lovely . . . forested hills around Nashville [became] . . . denuded of trees."[329] Southern soldier James Cooper revealed the extent of shoeless men in Hood's army whose "bloody tracks could be plainly seen on the ice and snow" and continued that "I had read of such things occurring during the Revolutionary War, but here were scenes eclipsing in suffering all . . . I had ever imagined."[330] A private in Bate's division summoned up an image of Promethean misery, "We had to take the weather like a lot of beasts."[331]

McKinney comments that by December 9, the future of Thomas's military career hung by a very thin thread because that day saw Grant write his second order relieving him of command. Halleck, feeling some misgivings, delayed sending it until after discussion with Lincoln and Stanton. Three and a half hours later, he informed Grant that neither the president nor the secretary of war felt good about removing Thomas. He explained that it would be up to Grant to issue the order or not and that responsibility for the order would be entirely his. At this, the general-in-chief balked, asking instead that Halleck prod Thomas with a reminder about how important immediate action had become.[332]

Halleck's wire of the 9th, informing Thomas of Grant's great "dissatisfaction" may have given Thomas his first clear glimpse into Grant's mind. He steadfastly informed Halleck that, though he regretted General Grant's feelings, he remained convinced that he had done everything possible to prepare and further that "the

---

[326] Ibid., 114-115.

[327] Groom, *Shrouds of Glory*, 233.

[328] OR: I: XLV: II, 115.

[329] Groom, *Shrouds of Glory*, 238.

[330] Ibid.

[331] Ibid., 239.

[332] McKinney, *Education in Violence*, 400.

troops could not have been gotten ready before this."[333] Thomas concluded, telling Halleck plainly that the storm would "render and attack impossible until it breaks."[334] For Thomas, advancing during such inclement conditions would result in unnecessary loss of life among his men. Perhaps Grant had lost sight of what had happened when he committed his troops to an ill-advised assault at Cold Harbor back in June. In his wire to Grant, Thomas patiently explained the restrictions imposed by severe weather, reminded him that the navy carefully patrolled crossing points on the Cumberland, and concluded by stating simply, "I have done all in my power to prepare, and if you should deem it necessary to relieve me, I shall submit without a murmur."[335] Thomas would not be pushed.

The powerful storm raging through Tennessee locked both secessionist and unionist forces in place. Grant, however, continued to fear a Confederate march through Kentucky. Should such a thing succeed, the war could be extended indefinitely. Grant sensed a vulnerable enemy and looked for the knock-out punch. Thomas, despite continued pressure from his chief, held firm. According to Van Horne, "Thomas preferred to be relieved rather than be responsible for battle fought under unfavorable conditions."[336] Unforeseen delays in equipping the army nullified Thomas's first projected date of attack, December 7, but two days later, he felt fully prepared. The cavalry at last stood ready, thanks to Wilson's strenuous efforts in stimulating "the inflows of new horses and . . . ransacking . . . corrals of convalescent animals."[337] Only nature stood in the way. Thomas sent out a reconnaissance on the 11th and 13th, but findings revealed that "infantry could move only with the greatest difficulty."[338] Attack during the days of December 9 to 14 would have made Union soldiers, slipping and sliding on the icy ground, easy targets for Hood's men standing securely behind their breastworks.

At an officers meeting on the eleventh, Thomas informed his men that Grant was being impatient and pushing for an attack. He also told them that he had decided to suspend any aggression until the storm cleared. The following day, he asked for a vote on the issue. Unanimously, his generals agreed about the danger and impracticality of assaulting the enemy under such conditions. One officer spoke for all, declaring, "The men cannot walk, sir. If they cannot walk, they cannot advance upon the enemy."[339] Another commented on Hood's situation, "We can be assured

---

[333]   OR: I: XLV: II, 114.

[334]   Ibid.

[335]   Ibid., Note: At Cold Harbor, Grant lost nearly seven thousand men in less than an hour. For further reading, see Ernest B. Furgurson, *Not War but Murder: Cold Harbor 1864* (New York: Alfred Knopf, 2000), 136-154.

[336]   Van Horne, *History of the Army of the Cumberland,* Volume II, 225.

[337]   Van Horne, *History of the Army of the Cumberland,* Volume II, 225.

[338]   Ibid., 50.

[339]   Buell, *The Warrior Generals,* 401.

that Hood shall neither attack us nor part our company to go to Ohio as General Grant . . . [fears] he might. He will stay where he is as we must."[340] Buell writes that Thomas did not report this meeting to his superiors. "Those in the East had no need to know what his generals had said, for suspicious minds might construe the meeting as conspiracy to disobey General Grant."[341]

As the meeting ended, Thomas asked Wilson to remain and remarked, "They [meaning General Grant and the War Department] treat me as though I were a boy . . . incapable of planning a campaign or fighting a battle. If they will let me alone, I will fight . . . just as soon as it can be done and will surely win it, but I will not throw the victory away nor sacrifice the brave men of the army by moving till the thaw begins." Finally, he declared, "I will not act against my judgment when I know I am right and in such a grave emergency."[342] Clearly, Thomas possessed full confidence in his ability, assessment of the military situation, and the potential human cost of hasty action.

When word got out to the soldiers that Thomas might be replaced, open "threats of revolt" ensued. Thomas attempted to smooth the troubled waters by telling his men "the government at Washington has a heavy task at hand. It has done the best it could under the circumstances."[343] Nevertheless, a defiant mood among the troops persisted as embodied by a remark heard among the ranks: "This is Old Pap's fight, and we are going to win it for him."[344]

Between the two meetings, Grant ordered Thomas to attack and ignore the weather. "If you delay attack any longer, the mortifying spectacle will be witnessed of a rebel army moving for the Ohio River," Grant charged, "and you will be forced to act, accepting such weather as you find. Let there be no further delay."[345] Clearly, Grant's impatience blinded him to realities on the ground and made him careless of the lives of men under someone else's command. Captain Henry Coupee, who had known Thomas since his West Point teaching days, summed the situation up well: "A weaker man than Thomas would have yielded to the importunity and attacked before he was ready."[346] Success and the welfare of his troops stood foremost in Thomas's mind, but he also knew that if things ended badly, he would shoulder the blame.

---

[340]   Ibid.

[341]   Ibid.

[342]   Major General James Harrison Wilson, "The Union Cavalry in the Hood Campaign" in *Battles and Leaders of the Civil War,* Volume IV (New York: The Century Company, 1884, 1888), 467.

[343]   McKinney, *Education in Violence,* 402.

[344]   Ibid., 403.

[345]   OR: I: XLV: II, 143.

[346]   Henry Coupee, *General Thomas* (New York: Appleton, 1897), 262, in Bobrick, *Master of War,* 287.

Besides pressure from above, Thomas faced an enemy within. In a detailed article, which appeared in the *Cincinnati Enquirer* after the war, General Steedman wrote that by December 12, Thomas had become suspicious that someone was sending denigrating messages to General Grant. Thomas's chief of staff, General Whipple, entertained similar thoughts. Bobrick writes that Steedman sent an aide to investigate the matter at the telegraph office. Once there, he found a message reading, "Many officers here are of the opinion that General Thomas is certainly too slow."[347] When Thomas saw the incriminating evidence, he recognized Schofield's handwriting. It made perfect sense. He served as Thomas's second-in-command and would take over should his chief be dismissed.[348]

On December 13, Grant stopped sending messages to Thomas; apparently, he had run out of patience. Halleck, however, tried a new tactic. He wrote that delay at Nashville kept troops under General Canby occupied in preventing reinforcements getting to Hood from the Trans-Mississippi. Canby, Halleck remarked, should have been joining General Sherman's forces in Georgia.[349] In other words, Halleck hinted that Thomas's intransigence was holding up Sherman's progress in Georgia. Ironically, Grant and Halleck seemed more concerned about Sherman, marching virtually unopposed toward Savannah, than Thomas who faced the Confederacy's second largest army at Nashville. As for Thomas, he spent little time in his reply to Halleck, remarking on the fourteenth: "The ice having melted away today; the enemy will be attacked tomorrow morning. Much as I regret the apparent delay in attacking . . . it could not have been done before with any remarkable hope of success."[350] During this crucial period, Confederate saboteurs cut the telegraph lines, and this important message did not reach Washington until the night of the fifteenth.

On the evening of December 13, Grant sent General John "Black Jack" Logan to Nashville with sealed orders to remove Thomas from command. If Thomas had not attacked by the time he arrived, he had permission to supersede him. Here, one wonders how Schofield would have reacted had this taken place. Apparently, Grant lacked confidence in his taking over command.

Following Logan's departure, Grant began to feel "restless" about the arrangements and decided to go to Tennessee himself.[351] As he had at Chattanooga in 1863 and with Mead's Army of the Potomac in 1864, Grant sought to take over. He left for Washington to confer with Lincoln and Stanton on the morning the 14th. Confronted with Grant's decision, both men objected, but the general-in-chief had

---

[347]   Bobrick, *Master of War,* 287.

[348]   McKinney, *Education in Violence,* 403; Bobrick, *Master of War,* 287.

[349]   OR: I: XLV: II, 180.

[350]   OR: I: XLV: II, 180.

[351]   Grant, *Personal Memoirs of U. S. Grant, Selected Letters 1839-1865* (New York: Literary Classics of the United States, Inc. 1990), 660.

his way. According to Bobrick, Lincoln tried to talk Grant out of the idea, arguing that "Thomas on the ground was better able to judge the situation than Grant far away."[352] Halleck and Stanton agreed, but Grant, terrier-like, held his ground and drew up an order relieving Thomas of command. Unbeknownst to Washington, however, the Battle of Nashville had already begun.

While Grant prepared to travel South, a great drama unfolded in middle Tennessee. The fourteenth saw a rise in temperature, and "a warm rain [clear] away the ice."[353] Battle orders sent by Thomas to the Fourth Corps encompass those sent out to his entire army: "Orders of the day for . . . tomorrow, December 15, 1864. Reveille will be sounded at 4:00 a.m. The troops will get their breakfast, break up their camps, pack up everything, and be prepared to move at 6:00 a.m."[354] The dramatic change in weather prompted swift action.

After his discussion with Lincoln and Stanton, Grant handed his third order removing Thomas from command to the government's chief telegraph officer, Major Thomas T. Eckert. Eckert knew that the telegraph lines had been down and thus held back Grant's order on his own responsibility, thinking it best to see what had happened. At 11:00 p.m., he found the lines open and began to review missing communications.[355]

The first message to come through was Thomas's reply to Halleck that he would attack in the morning, now a full twenty-four-hour-old. The next communication came from Van Duzer and dramatically described the success of the day: "Our line advanced and engaged the rebel line at nine this morning." He added, "The artillery practice has been fine, and at times, the musketry . . . continuous and heavy . . . though causalities have been light, the results are very fair."[356] The next wire, received at 11:25 from Thomas to Halleck, revealed the damage to Hood's army.

> "I attacked the enemy's left this morning and drove it from the river, below the city, very nearly to the Franklin Pike a distance about eight miles," Thomas related. "The troops behaved splendidly, all taking their share in assaulting and carrying the enemy's breastworks. I shall attack the enemy again tomorrow, if he stands to fight . . . and if he retreats . . . will pursue him throwing a heavy cavalry force in his rear to destroy his trains.[357]

The electrifying news prompted Eckert to rush outside with Grant's order still in his pocket, where he hailed an ambulance, "the 1864 counterpart of an official car"

---

[352]   Bobrick, *Master of War*, 289.

[353]   Bobrick, *Master of War*, 289.

[354]   OR: I: XLV: II, 185, 64.

[355]   Bobrick, *Master of War*, 289; McKinney, *Education in Violence*, 401-402.

[356]   OR: I: XLV: II, 196.

[357]   OR: I: XLV: II, 194.

and headed to Stanton's house.[358] Once there, he banged on the door. A window went up, and Stanton stuck his head out asking "What news?" "Good News!" Eckert replied and recalled later that he could hear Stanton's wife and children shouting "Hurrah!" from inside.[359]

Accompanied by the Secretary of War, Major Eckert directed the ambulance toward the White House. On the way, he revealed to Stanton that he never sent Grant's order. Stanton assured him he had made the right decision. After entering the darkened White House, Eckert beheld "the tall ghostly form of Lincoln in his night dress, with a lighted candle in his hand, as he appeared at the head of the second story landing . . . ."[360] Overjoyed, he too agreed that Eckert had done the right thing.

When he received a copy of Van Duzer's message at his hotel, Grant stated that he would not go to Nashville. In his memoirs, Grant remarked that his decision not to journey South rested upon Thomas's reply of the fourteenth to Halleck in which he said he declared his intention to attack the next morning.[361] However, with telegraph communications down, this was impossible. Eckert did not receive that message until after 11:00 p.m. on the fifteenth, several hours after Grant's meeting with Lincoln and Stanton. In truth, Grant decided not to go to Tennessee only after receiving overwhelming evidence of Thomas's success. As with many postwar writings, time blurred the facts.

In writing his memoirs, Grant may have suffered a memory lapse, understandable given his battle with acute throat cancer at the time. In addition, he possibly felt embarrassed by or regretted his overreaction, even years later. Indeed, others expressed similar feelings: Writing in 1887, Colonel Henry Stone, who served on Thomas's staff, recalled Grant's badgering of Thomas as "a story too painful to dwell upon, even after [a] lapse of twenty-three years."[362] What explains Grant's behavior? His biography reveals a life punctuated by failure. He tasted its bitter dregs following the war with Mexico and again in the wake of the Battle of Shiloh in 1862. At that time, General Henry Halleck took over Grant's army and placed Grant in a supernumerary post. While his title sounded impressive, he held few real responsibilities. Halleck seemed intent on making Grant perform penance for Shiloh's first day. He placed Thomas in command of Grant's old troops, creating a burning resentment in Grant's mind.[363] It is possible Grant begrudged Thomas and that this contributed to his condescending messages during the lead up to Nashville. Fate and ambition had combined to give Thomas something he had long desired,

[358] McKinney, *Education in Violence*, 402.

[359] Buell, *The Warrior Generals*, 402; OR: I: XLV: II, 196.

[360] Ibid., 403.

[361] Grant, *Personal Memoirs of U. S. Grant*, 660.

[362] Stone, "Repelling Hood's Invasion of Tennessee" in *Battles and Leaders,* volume IV, 454.

[363] McKinney, *Education in Violence*, 138-139; Bobrick, *Master of War*, 199-200.

an independent command. More importantly, Nashville gave him a chance to prove himself. Grant may well have resented this opportunity for greatness. Something dark lay behind his treatment of a man who had repeatedly demonstrated loyalty to the Union along with extraordinary military acumen.

Another contributing factor may have been the tense mood of the country; the nation's attention focused itself upon the government, General-in-Chief Grant, who had been mired down in front of Petersburg for over six months and the developing crisis in Tennessee. Grant, despite initial reservations, nevertheless approved Sherman's plan to march to Savannah with a well-equipped army of sixty thousand, while a dangerous foe remained upon the field in Tennessee. Perhaps Grant, who always remained attuned to public opinion, felt additional pressure for action. In many ways, Sherman left Thomas to pick up the pieces. Bobrick argues that by leaving Tennessee vulnerable, Grant and Sherman "blundered on a colossal scale."[364] Had Thomas not been so capable and had Hood succeeded in taking Nashville and crossing the Cumberland into Kentucky, the Union's top two generals would have looked foolish indeed. United States General R. W. Johnson commented that Southern success at that time could have delayed "the closing scenes of the war for years."[365] Ironically for Grant, the man he treated with such disdain contributed largely to securing his military reputation and subsequent political career. Notably, Thomas receives little thanks in Grant's memoirs, only comments about his "slowness."[366] Grant seemed unwilling to give the Virginian the credit he deserved.

When it became clear that Hood intended to attack Nashville and the situation reached a boiling point, Grant must have realized the risks inherent in Sherman's plan. He must have known too that if things turned out badly, he would also share the blame. Perhaps he felt determined not to allow failure to intrude upon his life again. Such pressure and mental questioning might explain the nagging, near-hysterical tone of Grant's messages. They also indicate, however, that he either underestimated or ignored Thomas's ability. Neither Grant nor anyone else, for that matter, was completely prepared for the responsibilities of being general-in-chief during a time of unique American crisis.[367]

December 16 confirmed a great Union victory in the West. President Lincoln sent Thomas a congratulatory wire but reminded him to finish the job. "Please accept for yourself, officers, and men the nation's thanks for your good work of yesterday. You made a magnificent beginning. A grand consummation is within your

---

[364]   Bobrick, *Master of War, 278.*

[365]   Ibid.

[366]   Grant, *Personal Memoirs of U. S. Grant,* 660-661.

[367]   For other critical comment regarding Grant's messages, see Van Horne, *History of the Army of the Cumberland,* volume II, 224-225; McKinney, *Education in Violence,* 399-403; Buell, *The Warrior Generals,* 398-403; Bobrick, *Master of War,* 278-279.

easy reach."[368] This message reflects not only memories of an incomplete victory at Gettysburg but also a pattern repeated throughout the war, one where Confederate forces had been defeated in battle but allowed to escape and fight another day. Thomas answered, assuring Lincoln that not only had more success been achieved but that his plans included destruction of Hood's army:

> The enemy has been pressed at all points today on his line of retreat . . . . McArthur's division [captured] sixteen pieces of artillery, two brigadier generals, and about two thousand prisoners . . . . I have ordered the pursuit to be continued at daylight, although the troops are very much fatigued. The greatest enthusiasm prevails . . . . The woods, fields, and entrenchments are strewn with the enemy's small arms, abandoned in their retreat . . . . I am happy to state that all this has been effected with but very small loss to us . . . . [it] does not probably exceed three thousand; very few killed.[369]

The victory in Tennessee immediately lifted morale, especially in Virginia, where Union troops had been engaged in exhausting trench warfare. Grant's chief-of-staff, General Rawlins, wired his boss from Petersburg, "If you have any further news of General Thomas' success, will you please send it, as it inspires the army here with great enthusiasm."[370]

Unionist civilians living near the Tennessee capital beset with anxiety and tired of bloodshed, expressed great relief. Maggie Lindsey wrote in her diary, "Sunday again and with it, peace and quiet. The battle is over. Confederates have retreated, General Thomas pursuing . . . . Glorious Thomas! (I cannot speak his name without tears, and from that, I know I am pretty well shattered by all recent excitement.) Countless blessings on his noble head!"[371] It appeared at last that the end of war might be in sight. Union victory at Nashville had done more than defeat an army; it had shattered Confederate resistance in the West.

[368]   OR: I: XLV: II, 210.

[369]   OR: I: XLV: II, 210.

[370]   Ibid., 212.

[371]   Buell, *The Warrior Generals*, 403.

CHAPTER 5

Battle and Retreat

The Battle of Nashville stood as an example of tactical excellence well into the twentieth century, providing inspiration for future army officers at West Point as well as military schools in Europe.[372] General Thomas's plan of feinting to the right, while delivering a crushing blow to the enemy's left, succeeded brilliantly on both days. The Union commander's ultimate goal had been to use a combination of cavalry and infantry to pursue, encircle, and destroy the rebel force during the battle's aftermath. Logistical problems, a Confederate head start, and determined resistance carried out by the Southern rear guard prevented realization of this aim, dissatisfying critics in Washington. Thomas did succeed, however, in severely damaging Hood's army while literally driving it out of Tennessee. It would later surface like flotsam from a terrible storm in Tupelo, Mississippi, in early January, its ragged ranks no longer capable of halting the Union tide in the West.

As the morning of December 15 dawned, thick fog shrouded the lines of both armies. Combined with undulations in the ground, the mist made it possible for Union troops to execute preparatory movements without detection but also made it impossible to attack at 6:00 a.m. as originally planned. When the atmosphere finally cleared around noon, Hood's army experienced an unpleasant revelation. As Historian Thomas Van Horne notes, up to this point in his campaign, Hood had monopolized the offensive, but now the tables had turned. Because Union troops on the Confederate right had "continually made the pretense of aggression" in the ten days leading up to battle, Hood found himself unprepared for a heavy blow to his left. Thomas had planned exactly that strategy.[373] Indeed, Confederate messages show that as late as December 10, Hood remained unsure of where the fighting would take place. Would it be along the lines presently occupied by his army, or somewhere else? In a circular issued that day, Hood mentioned a high probability of battle "before the close of the present year," but he added that "should it occur in front of Nashville, . . . corps commanders [should] send all . . . wagons except

---

[372]   Horn, *The Decisive Battle of Nashville,* Preface, v.
[373]   Van Horne, *History of the Army of the Cumberland,* Volume II, 229-230.

artillery, ordnance, and ambulances to the vicinity of Brentwood [on the Franklin Pike and about fourteen miles South] to go into park."[374] Clearly, Hood not only wished to protect his wagon train but also to be prepared for the possibility of retreat.

On the thirteenth Hood received information that Union cavalry had been crossing the Cumberland and pouring into Nashville from Edgefield. In response, he directed General Stewart to increase infantry presence on the Hardin Pike from a regiment to a brigade.[375] He could have taken this as positive indication that Thomas had at last assembled his cavalry force, boding ill for Hood in the near future. Instead, historian Winston Groom comments that as late as early morning of the fifteenth, "Hood . . . still [cranked] out telegrams to various authorities in the rear, trying to reclaim detached troops and other things for his army."[376] Other messages from that morning show that all important redoubts (self-supporting forts manned by artillery and infantry) along his battle line remained under construction.[377] In short, Hood was still preparing for a future battle on the day it struck. Other than cavalry movements, he had been deceived by the secrecy of Thomas's preparations.

Union Major General James Steedman, known affectionately as "Old Chickamauga" for heroic action at that battle, advanced an aggressive feint on Hood's right as soon as the mists cleared. Not meant to be a real attack, Steedman's movement nevertheless contained enough "spirit and force [to be] mistaken for a positive assault."[378] Though formally designated as a corps, the Union's Provisional Detachment of the District of the Etowah consisted of a mixed bag of "garrison soldiers, stragglers, deserters, quartermaster troops, and detached and unattached units."[379] It also contained eight regiments of black troops who had yet to fight in brigade formation.

This body of troops went into action against veteran soldiers commanded by Benjamin Franklin Cheatham and quickly suffered significant casualties. Though they failed to achieve a breakthrough, they succeeded in keeping the Confederates occupied on their right. Union Colonel Henry Stone wrote that the very presence of Steedman's men "kept two divisions of Cheatham's corps constantly busy."[380] Stone further noted that Union General Thomas J. Wood's corps (formally commanded by David Stanley, wounded at Franklin), along with "the threatening position of [Nashville's] garrison troops," kept Confederate General S. D. Lee's corps in

---

374   OR: I: XLV: II, 672.

375   Ibid., 686.

376   Groom, *Shrouds of Glory*, 242.

377   OR: I: XLV: II, 690-691.

378   Van Horne, *History of the Army of the Cumberland*, 230.

379   Groom, *Shrouds of Glory*, 242.

380   Colonel Henry Stone, "Repelling Hood's Invasion of Tennessee," in *Battles and Leaders Series*. Volume IV, 457.

position and rendered them ineffectual.[381] After sending reinforcements to General Stewart on the Confederate left, the remainder of Cheatham and Lee's troops "were held as in a vise between Steedman and Wood."[382]

Nashville presented one of the few Civil War battlefields with full visibility where opposing commands could clearly see each other's movements. Hood quickly perceived that the Union's main thrust would come on his left. Moving troops from Cheatham and Lee's corps to better solidify Stewart's position of the line took time, however, and they arrived too late to have the desired effect. Though Thomas's deception did not last long, it nonetheless bought enough time to ensure a successful result.

Thomas next launched a grand right wheel against Hood's left. As troops from the Confederate right attempted to aid their comrades, Hatch's dismounted cavalry, and A. J. Smith's corps bent Hood's line back beyond the Hillsboro Pike toward Montgomery Hill. Both Cheatham and Lee, unable to resist heavy Union pressure, fell back. Like most competent generals, Hood had prepared for such an eventuality, and Stewart's men moved into prepared entrenchments and took cover behind a stone wall that extended along most of the new position. Here, Hood had made sure that elevations "in front of this line . . . [were] crowned by a series a redoubts."[383] Though formidable in design and supposed to be virtually impregnable, these forts, as previously noted, remained under construction and incomplete when Thomas's powerful assault came rolling across the fields. Though Stewart extended his line to utmost tension, he lacked the manpower to cover redoubts four and five. Slowly but certainly, as Union pressure increased, the entire Confederate line started to crumble.[384]

Confederate commanders regarded the unfolding situation with trepidation. Soon, nervous messages began to be exchanged. Brigadier General Claudius Sears told Stewart, "A heavy column of infantry is moving to our left." Colonel Robert Lowery warned Major General Loring that "there seems to be a movement of some magnitude to our left." Finally, Colonel W. D. Gale reported that "the demonstration of the enemy on our left is increasing."[385] Stewart felt the full impact of this last because it meant he was in the process of being flanked. One by one, the redoubts fell, and four and five collapsed first. With these obstacles removed, the Union artillery turned its attention to gray troops crouching behind the stone wall, two brigades from Lee's corps. While the men kept down behind

[381]   Colonel Henry Stone, "Repelling Hood's Invasion of Tennessee," in *Battles and Leaders Series*. Volume IV, 457.

[382]   Ibid.

[383]   Groom, *Shrouds of* Glory, 245; Mark Zimmerman, *Guide to Civil War Nashville* (Nashville: Battle of Nashville Preservation Society, 2004), 54-55.

[384]   Groom, *Shrouds of Glory*, 245.

[385]   OR: I: XLV: II, 692.

the rapidly disintegrating barrier, Union Brigadier General John A. McArthur's troops advanced, accelerating into a charge and raising a cheer that shattered the Confederate line. Despite attempts by Cheatham and Lee's men to stem the Union tide, Stewart felt compelled to withdraw. In his post battle report, he complained bitterly that at this point, the troops put up "but feeble resistance [and] fled."[386] He further stated that he found it impossible to "check the progress of the enemy who had passed the Hillsboro Pike a full half-mile, completely turning our flank, and gaining the rear of both Walthall and Loring whose situation [had become] perilous to the extreme."[387]

Commentary indicates that relentless pressure from Thomas caused Confederate morale to collapse. W. D. Gale, General Stewart's adjutant, had an uncomfortably close encounter with the Union deluge. Gale, whose job it had been to send messages from a house near Hillsboro Pike, wrote, "I mounted and made my escape through the backyard with my clerks. As our men fell back before the advancing Yankees," he continued, "Mary Bradford [a neighborhood girl] ran out under heavy fire and did all she could to induce the men to stop and fight, appealing to them and begging them but in vain . . . . I never witnessed such a want of enthusiasm and begin to fear for tomorrow."[388] Civilians had one view, but soldiers had another. After enduring weeks of freezing wet weather, a shortage of such basic supplies as shoes and blankets and burdened by terrible fatigue, many men simply reached the end of their endurance. For them, Thomas's steamroller attack proved the last straw.

As Confederate lines deteriorated, the Yankee attack unfolded with precision and according to plan. Thomas asked Union Cavalry Commander James Harrison Wilson's men to perform three tasks: take part as infantry in the initial assault upon Confederate lines, protect the Union right flank, and when opportunity presented itself, to mount their horses, sweep around Hood's flank, and harass and infiltrate the Confederate rear. They performed these tasks with élan and proved Thomas correct in waiting for his cavalry to become fully equipped.[389] With Forrest still engaged with Rousseau's force at Murfreesboro, the task of stopping Wilson's men fell to Confederate General James Chalmers's cavalry. Though outnumbered several times to one, they resisted gallantly until finally pushed back late in the afternoon. Confederate spirit, in the end, proved no match for Union power.

---

[386] Groom, *Shrouds of Glory*, 247.

[387] Ibid., 248.

[388] Gale and Polk Family Papers, Southern Historical Collection, UNC, in Brian Craig Miller, *John Bell Hood and the Fight for Civil War Memory* (Knoxville, University of Tennessee Press, 2010), 161.

[389] Van Horne, *History of the Army of the Cumberland*. Volume II, 231-232; Stone, "Repelling Hood's Invasion of Tennessee," 459.

In the midst of the carnage and gunfire, a woman once again demonstrated Southern determination. While following orders to save Chalmer's wagon train, Lieutenant James Dinkins encountered hundreds of Union troops swarming around Belle Meade plantation house (a local landmark then, as now) where he discovered that the train had already been destroyed. Distressed, Dinkins and Chalmers's now-skeletonized escort determined to cut their way out and avoid capture. Achieving surprise at first, they ran up against a strong line of Yankee infantry and retreated back past Belle Meade. While "bullets . . . [clipped] the shrubbery and [struck] the house," Dinkins recalled, he noticed Ms. Selene Harding waving her handkerchief from the mansion's front steps while enthusiastically encouraging fleeing Confederates to stand and fight. Dinkins wrote that "she looked like a goddess," adding that "she was the gamest little human in all the crowd."[390] Civilians had not endured the privations experienced by the troops; therefore, their morale seems to have outlasted that of Confederate soldiers.

After sunset, Hood withdrew to a new position, approximately two miles from where his army had stood at noon. The secessionists reorganized themselves into a line, shaped like an elongated *C*. On the left, it anchored on Compton's Hill, a site later renamed by Union troops as Shy's Hill, after Confederate Colonel William Shy who died defending it. At 2.5 miles in length, considerably shorter than Hood's original line, it had much stronger defensive potential. Wilson wrote that the Confederate position, masked by "thick woods and undergrowth of the Brentwood Hills," made it appear almost impregnable.[391] Stone added that its flanks were protected by "return works" constructed during the night, preventing them (at least in theory) from being "left in the air."[392] Hood repositioned his generals with Chalmers cavalry defending the far left (West sector), Cheatham the upper left (curve of the elongated *C* set around Shy's Hill), Stewart at the center, and S. D. Lee covering Stewart's right and the far right set on Overton's Hill. They faced Union generals Wilson on the far right (facing Cheatham and Chalmers), Schofield (facing most of Cheatham's corps and Shy's Hill), A. J. Smith on Schofield's left covering the center along with T. J. Wood, and Steedman stationed on the extreme left.

On December 16, with his usual attention to detail, Thomas prepared to destroy Hood's army by sending out skirmishers to ascertain the true position of the rebel lines. Armed with this intelligence, his army prepared for another attack. By 8:00 a.m., they stood ready for action. At about this time, though fully intending to fight from his new line, Hood sent contingency plans to General Stewart should a reverse

---

[390]   Groom, *Shrouds of Glory*, 249-250.

[391]   Wilson, "The Union Cavalry in the Hood Campaign," in *Battles and Leaders Series*. Volume IV, 469.

[392]   Stone, "Repelling Hood's Invasion of Tennessee," 460.

occur. It seems certain that he reflected on Thomas's strengths and results of the previous day:

> Should any disaster happen to us today . . . . you will retire by the Franklin
> Pike, and Lee is directed to hold it in front of this large ridge [Overton's
> Hill and other elevations] that you may pass to his rear. After passing
> Brentwood, you would again form your corps in the best position you can
> find and let the whole army pass through you. There are some narrow
> gorges beyond Brentwood toward Franklin. At all times, the roads must
> be left open for artillery and wagons, the men marching though the fields
> and woods.[393]

Well aware of his army's weakness, Hood laid the ground for a possible fighting retreat. Once the army went past Brentwood, about twelve miles southward, road conditions would make it extremely difficult to flank troops defended by a determined rear guard.

Meanwhile, Thomas pursued a plan similar to that used the previous day. He sent Steedmans's troops to attack the East section (extreme right) of Hood's line, hoping it would cause the Confederate commander to remove troops from his left, Thomas's major objective. There, Wilson's dismounted cavalry would work their way around the West sector and move to the enemy's rear. Once that happened, causing panic in the rebel ranks, Thomas would launch a heavy attack on Shy's Hill. This, he felt, would cause collapse of the Confederate line. Throughout the day, Union artillery battered Hood's lines relentlessly.

By noon, Steedman's men, having run into stiff opposition, found themselves stymied. They had experienced no success in dislodging S. D. Lee. By 10:00 a.m., Wilson's troops had suffered a similar fate, and Wilson asked Thomas if he might move his command over to the Confederate right and try his luck there. The more patient Thomas told him to keep at it where he was. Two hours later, Union cavalrymen finally began to move around the enemy's left and in behind Cheatham. At this time, Wilson's men captured a frantic message from Hood to Cheatham: "For God's sake, [drive] the Yankee cavalry from our left and rear or all is lost."[394] Wilson felt that the time had come for Schofield to attack Cheatham's position, sending three couriers, one after another, to tell Thomas. Schofield, however, at this major turning point, hesitated and expressed anxiety about the dangers of an assault. In addition, he feared that Hood might actually attack him. Noting that Schofield's men had not moved, and feeling strongly that a decisive opportunity might be lost, Wilson rode in person to Thomas's command post. There, in a state

---

[393]   OR: I: XLV: II, 696.

[394]   Groom, *Shrouds of Glory*, 257; Wilson, "The Union Cavalry in the Hood Campaign," *Battles and Leaders Series*. Volume IV, 469.

of "ill concealed impatience," he found Thomas remonstrating with the recalcitrant Schofield. In response to fears that attacking Hood might be costly, Thomas replied, "the battle must be fought even if men are killed."[395] By this time at 4:00 p.m., the day had grown dark, and opportunity threatened to slip away. Fortunately, General McArthur, whose division formed part of A. J. Smith's corps on Schofield's left, decided to assault Shy's Hill without orders from Thomas. In observing the Confederate position, McArthur noticed that rebel commanders had placed both artillery and infantry incorrectly. They stood on the true crest rather than the military crest which is somewhat lower and affords opportunity to fire into attackers. In short, Cheatham's men on Shy's Hill had been placed too far back to be effective. Seeing McArthur's men carrying the Confederate position, Thomas turned to Schofield and announced coldly, "General Smith [meaning McArthur's division] is attacking without waiting for you . . . please advance with your entire line."[396] Like the attack by Thomas's men carried out in defiance of General Grant's orders at Missionary Ridge in 1863, this one also shattered the Confederate position. Stone writes,

> The bravest onlookers held their breath as these gallant men steadily . . . approached the summit amid the crash of musketry and the boom of artillery. In almost the time it has taken to tell the story, they gained the works; their flags wildly waving from the parapet, and the unmistakable cheer, "The voice of the American people," as General Thomas called it, rent the air.[397]

At the time McArthur's men made their assault, elements of Wilson's cavalry forced significant inroads into the Confederate rear: "With incredible labor, they . . . dragged by hand, two pieces of artillery . . . and these opened up on" the reverse side of Shy's Hill.[398] In addition, Coon's cavalry brigade (of Hatch's division) charged the now beleaguered rebels, pouring in rapid volleys with their repeating rifles. Beset on two sides, Confederate defenders "broke out of [their] works and ran down the hill toward . . . their rear as fast as their legs could carry them. It was more like a scene in a spectacular drama than a real incident in war."[399] Word of collapse on the left ran through Hood's ranks like wildfire, resulting in disintegration of the entire battle line. Many years later, Hood recalled Shy's Hill with simple clarity: The enemy "made a sudden and gallant charge up to and over our entrenchments. Our line, thus pierced, gave way; soon, there after it broke at all points, and I beheld for the

---

[395]   Ibid.; Van Horne, *History of the Army of the Cumberland,* 239-240.

[396]   Wilson, "The Union Cavalry in the Hood Campaign," 469; Stone, "Repelling Hood's Invasion of Tennessee," 463; Groom, *Shrouds of Glory,* 258.

[397]   Stone, "Repelling Hood's Invasion of Tennessee," 463.

[398]   Ibid.

[399]   Ibid., 464.

first and only time a Confederate army abandon the field in confusion." He added that he "soon discovered that all hope to rally the troops was in vain."[400]

After nearly two months of enduring inhuman weather conditions, a serious lack of basic items of comfort, such as clothing, shoes, and blankets and an ever-tightening supply line, men of the Army of Tennessee reached their breaking point. A member of the United States Christian Commission, after seeing the condition of Confederate prisoners, stated that "Hood's army had endured fatigues and privations almost beyond belief."[401]

As Civil War battles go, the percentage of casualties was relatively low. "Thomas listed his [loses] at 3,061—387 killed, 2,562 wounded, and 112 missing . . . . Thomas also said . . . he captured 4,462 prisoners and fifty-three pieces of artillery," over half of the Army of Tennessee's total supply. As for Hood, his losses numbered less than a third of those lost at Franklin, at 2,300.[402] Edwin Stanton sent an enthusiastic wire to Major General Dix in New York recording Union success at Nashville. He declared, "One of the most surprising circumstances connected with this great achievement is the small loss suffered by our troops, evincing . . . the admirable skill and caution of General Thomas."[403] Despite Stanton and Grant's earlier criticisms of Thomas for failure to attack sooner, such commentary correctly recognizes his accurate assessment of the situation at hand.

At this point, Union cavalry encountered problems that prevented completion of its assigned task. Wilson states that in making their considerable contribution to the attack, as infantry equipped with rapidly firing weapons, the cavalry became unavoidably separated from their horses as they advanced. Nightfall arrived before full-scale pursuit could be organized. Nevertheless, officers Hatch, Knipe, Croxton, Hammond, Coon, and Spalding did their best to cut off the Franklin Pike, at that point, Hood's only remaining escape route. Another of Wilson's officers received orders to "move rapidly by the Hillsboro Turnpike and after crossing the Harpeth [River] to turn up its South bank and fall upon the enemy at or near Franklin."[404]

Hood's contingency plans from earlier in the day bore fruit as daylight faded. Secessionists reached strategically defensible sections along the Franklin Pike before Union troops could intervene; these were the "narrow gorges" that Hood had referred to in his message to Stewart that morning. Despite heroic efforts by Wilson's cavalry, Confederates achieved enough of a start to reach Franklin first, where Union cavalry under Colonel Spalding encountered Chalmer's gray horsemen situated behind hastily improvised barricades on the town's outskirts. The Union troopers charged and in "a spirited hand-to-hand mêlée . . . in which many . . . were

---

[400]   Hood, *Advance and Retreat*, 303.

[401]   Zimmerman, *Guide to Civil War Nashville*, 58.

[402]   Ibid., Also see Thomas's Report: OR: I: XLV: II, 210-211.

[403]   OR: I: XLV: II, 227-228.

[404]   Wilson, "The Union Cavalry in the Hood Campaign," 469.

killed and wounded on each side" drove the enemy from their works.[405] Chalmers, nevertheless, succeeded in buying enough time for harassed comrades in the infantry to continue their escape. In a 3:00 a.m. message sent to Thomas on the 17th, Wilson noted that a captured dispatch from Hood to Chalmers proclaimed, "Time is all we want." He correctly interpreted this to mean that Hood "expects the arrival of Forrest's forces" coming from Murfreesboro.[406] Forrest would become the key to the rebel rear guard. At one in the afternoon, things had looked more promising, with Wilson wiring Thomas from Franklin, in a tone breathless with excitement:

> The rebels are on a great skedaddle; the last of them pressed by Knipe, passed through this place two hours and a half ago. I have directed Johnson to try and strike them at Spring Hill. Knipe is pressing down the Columbia Pike; Hatch close on their left; Croxton, I shall direct down the Lewisburg Pike. The prisoners report that rebel army in complete rout, and all the Tennesseans are deserting.[407]

Prior to this, on the night of the 16th, Wilson recalled being overtaken by General Thomas while galloping down the Granny White Pike: "It was so dark that men could recognize each other only by their voices. Thomas, riding up on my right, exclaimed in a tone of exultation never to be forgotten, "Didn't I tell you we could lick 'em if only they [Grant and the government] would leave us alone?"[408]

Forrest rejoined Hood's retreating army on the 19th, and Union cavalry engaged the Confederates in a series of sharp fights. Each day, as darkness fell, gray and blue battled one another in pitch blackness. Forrest, who assumed command of the rear guard, did his best to hold off fast pursuing and aggressive Union troops. This formed the pattern of fighting for several days. Eventually, "men and horses [became] ravenously hungry and almost worn out" from continuous combat. By the 19th, Thomas's cavalry found themselves almost out of rations, so far had they outpaced their wagon train. Nevertheless, the men felt consolation in knowing that they drove Confederate troops in far worse conditions than themselves.[409]

Efforts to keep the Southern army moving prompted desperate measures. In a circular directed to his officers at Pulaski on December 21, Hood issued orders aimed at preserving horses and mules:

> It is necessary that strong fatigue details, under energetic officers, should be placed with all [wagon] trains, and in cases of necessity, animals will

---

[405]   Ibid.

[406]   OR: I: XLV: II, 237.

[407]   OR: I: XLV: II, 237-238.

[408]   Wilson, "The Union Cavalry in the Hood Campaign," 469-470.

[409]   Ibid.

be taken from the wagons to draw the artillery, and the loads of army wagons will be partially or entirely thrown out to preserve the wagons and teams. Every possible exertion will be made to collect forage at this point, that teams may leave here with a supply which will be used as sparingly as possible. Battery commanders will have grass pulled for their animals wherever it can be found.[410]

He also ordered brigade commanders to unload "all the tool wagons of their . . . commands" and send them "down the Pulaski Pike three or four miles . . . [to] search diligently for forage and return with the least delay."[411] Even though such precautions slowed movement, draft animals had to be saved; without them, Hood would lose all of his artillery and supply wagons. This cannot have been easy in the bleak, frost-bitten Tennessee countryside with a determined enemy nipping at the army's heels. Hood also voiced concern for the condition of his men, directing Major General Carter Stevenson, to have the soldiers make "as good a day's march as possible without pushing the troops too much."[412] Despite efforts on both sides to care for troops' welfare, suffering escalated.

Evidence testifying to the desperate condition of Hood's men abounded. Sam Watkins, one Tennessean still with the army, noted his ragged comrades "with sunken cheeks and famine-glistening eyes."[413] He remarked that "our wagon trains had either gone on; we know not whither or had been left behind," revealing that Thomas's men had broken the rebel supply line.[414] At Franklin, Hood wrote the wounded Watkins a furlough, signaling his exit from the war. For Watkins, Hood embodied the condition of his army: "I remember when passing by Hood, how feeble and decrepit he looked, with an arm in a sling and a crutch in the other hand . . . trying to guide and control his horse . . . . I prayed in my heart that day for General Hood."[415] Like his army, Hood gave his all for a Confederacy that in many ways betrayed him. Southern political and military leaders arrogantly ignored the North's superiority in industrial production, railroad networks, and population in 1861, thinking that foreign aid or superior fighting spirit would win the war for them. Now in the waning days of 1864, such hubris seemed incredibly short-sighted.

During the days that Grant harangued Thomas about a Confederate army moving northward, Hood sent numerous messages to his superiors pleading for reinforcements and trying to improve a decaying supply line. On December 2, General Beauregard wired E. Kirby-Smith on Hood's behalf to ask for help from

---

[410]   OR: I: XLV: II, 719.

[411]   Ibid.

[412]   Ibid.

[413]   Watkins, *Company Aytch*, 205.

[414]   Watkins, *Company Aytch*, 205.

[415]   Ibid., 206.

the Trans-Mississippi. Outlining the desperate situation in Tennessee, Beauregard stated forcefully that either Smith should send Hood "two or more divisions or that you should at once threaten Missouri in order to compel the enemy to recall . . . reinforcements he is sending to General Thomas."[416] To prioritize these requests, Beauregard contacted Confederate President Jefferson Davis whose reply revealed much about Smith: "If General Smith can now act as suggested, it would be well . . . There is no objection to his being called on, but he has failed heretofore to respond to like necessities, and no pleas should be based on his compliance."[417] True to Davis's estimation, Beauregard received neither reply nor action from the Trans-Mississippi commander as late as December 15, the first day of battle. That Smith could not be induced to move, despite Hood's desperate situation and that Davis did not remove him, is indicative of how badly Confederate command structure had disintegrated by 1864.

Southern politicians failed to support much needed efforts at unity, as inconsistent and localized deployment of troops and materials undermined the war effort. For example, Georgia Governor Joseph Brown demanded that all Georgia militia remain within the borders of that state following Atlanta, and he won his case. Moreover, Georgia also held vast quantities of supplies, such as shoes and clothing, which Hood's men so desperately needed. Few of these items reached soldiers in Tennessee. Instead, they remained in Georgia for the use of its rather ineffectual militia, now grossly outmanned by Sherman's blue juggernaut. For example, on December 13, Hood wired Beauregard: "Major Ayer, chief quartermaster, informs me that Major Bridewell at Augusta, [Georgia] has fifty bales of blankets belonging to this army. Please have them sent forward at once . . . . The weather is severe . . . ."[418] Lieutenant General Richard Taylor, in charge of the Department of Alabama, Mississippi, and Eastern Louisiana, complained bitterly to Colonel George William Brent, assistant adjutant general, at Montgomery regarding citizens' complaints about "officers, acting under the orders of General Hood . . . seizing their good mules [and] substituting in their places worthless and broken-down animals." He declared that such behavior "by an officer commanding another army or department will not be recognized by me unless I am ordered to do so."[419] Though Taylor received several messages delineating the serious situation in Tennessee, he refused to act as part of a team. Such possessive attitudes were exemplified by Brown, Taylor, and Smith. Personal fiefdoms, be they state or military, took precedence over the whole and played a dominant role in the Confederacy's ultimate demise. Hood faced a tricky situation in any case, but he also did so without ample support from above and below, while material shortages directly affected morale.

---

[416]   OR: I: XLV: II, 639-640.

[417]   OR: I: XLV: II, 636.

[418]   Ibid., 685.

[419]   OR: I: XLV: II., 689.

During the first two weeks of December, Hood complained about problems with the rail transport's effect on his supply line. As late as the thirteenth, he wired Beauregard that "the quartermaster charged with rebuilding the railroad from Cherokee toward Decatur, still complains of not being able to obtain the necessary labor and material. Please give him the authority to impress at once all that is necessary."[420] That these pleas went unfulfilled, and Hood's army wanted for basic supplies as they froze in front of Nashville, offers clear testimony to decay spreading throughout the Confederacy. Moreover, on December 2, Beauregard sent a long and revealing message to General S. Cooper, adjutant and inspector General in Richmond. He stated that Hood's army stood "sadly in need of every description of military supplies—horses and mules for artillery and other transportation, blankets, clothing, bacon, etc., are needed" and noted that "this section has been drained of these supplies."[421] He also remarked that most of the soldiers in the Tennessee army had not been paid in nearly a year. Especially revealing were his comments regarding sheer lack of specie and his hope that government cotton could be used in exchange for military supplies held in various states. Incredibly, according to Beauregard, no one "whose powers should be ample and whose instructions should be full and clear"[422] seemed available to address and or take charge of these problems. Clearly, the Confederacy was bankrupt, and its organizational infrastructure collapsed. The foundation of states' rights ideology ultimately yielded a house built upon sand. States' rights thinking clouded the larger strategic vision of military department commanders like Richard Taylor. Confederate Generals, including Lee in Virginia and Hood in Tennessee, found that they no longer had material or logistical support. Hood's army, not only because of its precipitate defeat but also because of the climatic conditions it fought through in December of 1864, stands as a fit metaphor for the Confederacy. "And the rain descended and the floods came, and the winds blew and beat upon that house; and it fell; and great was the fall of it."[423]

Hood managed to guide his broken army to safety by finally crossing the Tennessee River at Bridgeport, Alabama, on Christmas Day. General Wilson points to three reasons for Hood's escape: First, the Confederates had possession of the pike while "threading . . . valleys, depressions, and gorges [which] offered many advantages to defense."[424] Second, blue troops often outran their supply train and had to wait in

---

[420]   Ibid., 685. See also December 2, Beauregard to Governor Joe Brown: "It is important to put in running order the railroad from West Point via Atlanta, to Augusta. Cannot you impress or otherwise obtain nine hundred Negroes to report to Major Hottle, . . . who has charge of the work? Prompt action is necessary." (640). Also December 6, Hood to Beauregard: "Please have the railroad repaired to Decatur as soon as possible." (653).

[421]   OR: I: XLV: II, 637.

[422]   Ibid.

[423]   Matthew: 7, 24-27, *Holy Bible-Concordance* (Oxford University Press), 738.

[424]   Wilson, "The Union Cavalry in the Hood Campaign," 471.

order to feed themselves and their tiring horses. Finally, credit must be given to Forrest for orchestrating a masterful rearguard defense. The badly wounded Confederate army remained dangerous, and Union troops felt wary of overcommitting in their flanking attempts. The retreat carried a heavy cost, according to Union Provost martial records and Forrest's own comments. Following the 175-mile pursuit, Union "cavalry captured 32 field guns, 11 caissons, 12 colors, 3332 prisoners, including one general officer, one train of 80 pontoons, and 125 wagons . . . Its own loses were one field gun, 122 officers and men killed, 521 wounded, and 259 missing."[425] During the first week of January, after the Union pursuit ended, Forrest remarked that in helping to save the Army during "retreat from Nashville I was compelled almost to sacrifice my command."[426] Though Thomas failed in one of his goals,—to encircle and entirely destroy Hood's army—Simpson writes that "his fierce . . . pursuit literally ran the Army of Tennessee out of the state."[427] It would never return.

Hood's narrow escape evoked dissatisfaction in Washington. Grant, the loudest critic, felt that the cavalry had been improperly used. He indicated that it would have been better utilized if the men had remained mounted, thus facilitating faster pursuit. General Wilson disagreed, stating emphatically that "the organization of the cavalry corps . . . during the progress of an active campaign, and in the presence of an invading army . . . from 4,500 to 12,000 mounted men . . . the successes it gained in battle, and the persistency with which it pursued the flying enemy, are without parallel in the history of this or any other war."[428] In connection to Grant's remarks about troops not fighting mounted, Wilson pointed out that the boggy and forested ground was unsuitable for mounted cavalry and that he used horses "upon that occasion, mainly for the transportation of the fighting men, and not to fight themselves . . . ."[429]

When Hood's beleaguered army arrived in Tupelo, Mississippi, on January 10, it numbered around fifteen thousand exhausted men. The Army of Tennessee could no longer threaten the Union. Forrest's much depleted cavalry departed, and several brigades went to Mobile, Alabama. The remaining five thousand men joined General Joe Johnston in North Carolina, where at Bentonville on March 19, 1865, Johnston ordered them into an assault on Union positions eerily reminiscent of the one carried out at Franklin. Hood, worn down like his army, did not wait to be relieved of command but submitted his resignation on January 23.[430] For the general, though fighting on the battlefield had ended, he would face another struggle in the years to come, this time for how he would be remembered in history.

---

[425] OR: I: XLV: II, 471.

[426] Ibid., 756.

[427] John A. Simpson, *Reminiscences of the Forty-First Tennessee*, 109.

[428] Wilson, "Union Cavalry in the Hood Campaign," 471.

[429] Ibid.

[430] Dyer, *The Gallant Hood*, 304.

CHAPTER 6

Through a Glass Darkly

The Civil War inflicted an unprecedented scale of death upon the nation with more soldier lives consumed than in all previous American wars combined. Such carnage disrupted, and even made irrelevant, certain aspects of traditional American death culture. In time, parallel mythologies developed to enable justification and acceptance of losses never before experienced. Southerners created what became known as the "Lost Cause," an ideology that has been well documented. Historian John R. Neff argues that Northerners countered with the "Cause Victorious," an ideology contending that the nation became more strongly unified as a result of the war. Both idea systems continue to exert strong historical and political influence. Lost Cause writers, in searching for ways to explain away defeat, sought scapegoats. Their efforts had a significant effect upon the historical memory of John Bell Hood.

Civil War fatalities, industrial in scale, overturned ritualized American death culture. For many citizens who attempted to find solace and order, it seemed as if chaos had descended upon society. By April 1865, total loss of life equaled two percent of the population of the United States. Of all combatants, nearly fourteen percent had been killed in action or died from related causes such as infection or disease. Neff uses the Vietnam War, another conflict that generated "great social strife," for modern comparison. Nearly sixty thousand U.S. service personnel died in connection with the war in Southeast Asia, totaling one percent of the national population, a sickening total. Yet "as a percentage . . . nearly 3.72 *million* soldiers would have to die—nearly sixty-five times the actual number killed—for Vietnam deaths to be on par with Civil War deaths."[431] Those of us who lived through the Vietnam years remember the trauma, anguish, and disgust elicited by the daily news reports of deaths of young military personnel. Neff makes the comparison to bring home the agony projected onto Americans living during the Civil War years. Taken alone, the Civil War has contributed nearly half (47.43 percent) of all military deaths

---

[431] John R. Neff, *Honoring the Civil War Dead: Commemoration and the Problems of Reconciliation* (Lawrence: University Press of Kansas, 2005), 20.

dating back to the Revolutionary War.[432] Torment did not end during the postwar years; veterans wounded both physically and emotionally acted as living reminders of the cost of war.

Prior to 1861, Americans developed and relied upon a well-defined ritual (death culture) to deal with personal loss. Death centered itself around the home; and essential elements included the deathbed, presence of family and friends at the hour of death, the body itself (washed and prepared for burial within the home), religious ceremony, and a procession to the local cemetery. Pursuit of a "good death" possessed great importance. A person "who remained conscious until the moment of death, resolute, even eager to submit to the end of life . . . gave evidence of an inward saving grace." Friends and relatives present at the deathbed gained inspiration and strength from the experience; they "literally learned how to die." Such customs eased people through the permanent separation represented by death.[433]

The Civil War shattered the cloak of security represented by antebellum death customs. Soldiers commonly died far from home, their deathbed (if any) attended by strangers. Many families had no knowledge of how their loved one died or assurance about the handling, condition, and location of the body. War presented harsh, even brutal reality. Too many young men found shallow graves in mud-filled holes, wrapped in a simple blanket or nothing at all. An unacceptable number of families would never locate the resting places of their sons or fathers. Harvard historian Drew Gilpin Faust writes that "nearly half of the dead remained unknown, the fact of their deaths supposed but undocumented, the circumstances of their passage from life entirely unrecorded." Thus, relatives and friends found it impossible to find closure as they "searched in anxiety . . . to provide endings for life narratives that stood incomplete, their meanings undefined."[434] Novelist and poet Herman Melville wrote about what soldiers encountered when they entered the Wilderness battlefield for the second time:

> In glades they meet skull after skull
> Where pine cones lay—the rusted gun,
> Green shoes full of bones; the mouldering coat
> And cuddled-up skeleton;
> And scores of such.[435]

---

[432]   Ibid.

[433]   Ibid., 23.

[434]   Drew Gilpin Faust, *This Republic of Suffering: Death and the American Civil War* (New York: Alfred A. Knopf, 2008), 267.

[435]   Herman Melville, "The Armies of the Wilderness" (1866) in Neff, *Honoring the Civil War Dead*, 16.

The miracle of modern photography allowed civilians to experience, at least vicariously, the horrors of the battlefield. "Newspapers listed the dead by name, but photographs *displayed* the violence."[436] The work of Matthew Brady and Alexander Gardner brought the dead soldier into American cities, almost as if he had been laid out along the sidewalks. Though Brady's display of "The Dead at Antietam" featured images of bloated bodies and distorted faces, others (in which newly dead bodies had been deliberately manipulated and "posed") attempted to show the deceased as sleeping peacefully as in Gardner's "The Home of the Rebel Sharpshooter, Gettysburg, July 1863." Historian Mark S. Schantz comments that photographers often tended to focus on landscapes in an attempt to show not only damage but also the peace that reigned after battles. By using such methods, Civil War photographers often tried to make a connection with antebellum death culture. [437]

From 1866 to 1869, the Federal government played a particularly active role in raising funds for development of national cemeteries. In the beginning, these housed almost exclusively Union soldiers. Bodies had to be disinterred from where they had been buried while battles raged and efforts at identification were made. Then the corpses were coffined and placed in a new national cemetery, usually not far from where the soldiers had actually died. The majority of the new national resting places lay in the South because that is where most of the battles had been fought. Neat rows of white stone markers, heroic statuary, and the presence of the Stars and Stripes combined to act as reminders of Southern defeat. Even in death, northern soldiers occupied Southern soil, representing an army that would never march away. Former rebels "concluded that the new cemeteries signified that they were second-class citizens within the new nation."[438]

No such efforts were made to gather, identify, and rebury Southern corpses that lay within the same battlegrounds. This would come later as would full development of memorialization activities related to Confederate Decoration Day. Despite the recognized need for reconciliation between North and South, particularly in the 1870s, an abiding animosity lingered. Neff argues that this had to do, in part, with unequal treatment of the dead following battle. Men belonging to the winning side tended to be buried first and with more care, with many graves being marked. The losers, on the other hand, found resting places in unmarked mass graves. If the army found it necessary to move on quickly, and many often did, some bodies might not be buried at all. Both sides shared these concerns, but northern victory helped ease much of the pain. Their unknown dead had at least fallen in a winning effort; nevertheless, knowledge of poor treatment of the dead bothered soldiers and

---

[436]   Neff, *Honoring the Civil War Dead*, 41.

[437]   Mark S. Schantz, *Awaiting the Heavenly Country* (Ithaca: Cornell University Press, 2008), 186-189.

[438]   William Blair, *Cities of the Dead: Contesting the Memory of the Civil War South, 1865-1914* (Chapel Hill: University of North Carolina Press, 2004), 53.

civilians of both regions. This engendered feelings of resentment and even outright anger to be directed at the other side. Looting or committing atrocities on corpses exacerbated the problem.[439]

Victorian social structure dictated that women take the leading role in cemetery memorialization activities. It can be argued that Southern women founded the Lost Cause "in the Spring of 1866" and that their "rituals . . . promised anything but reconciliation."[440] Republican politicians, noting the presence of former Confederate soldiers wearing their old uniforms, "saw an obstinate . . . people who threatened the hard-won achievements of the conflict."[441] Southerners defiantly displaying the Confederate flag at such ceremonies, no doubt felt marginalized by much larger Union-oriented celebrations featuring armed national troops, a significant number of which were black. To former Confederates, it seemed that Northerners resented efforts to honor rebel dead. By the end of the summer, federal regulations banned Confederate flags, symbols, uniforms, and in some cases, processions on national Decoration Day. Southerners had to honor their dead in a more restrained, almost secretive manner. Their time for celebration had not yet arrived.

An incident at Arlington National Cemetery in 1869 sharply revealed that for many Northerners, reconciliation remained unacceptable. The former estate of Robert and Mary Custis Lee had been converted into a national cemetery following the war, and bodies of Confederate soldiers, "many of whom had died while in prison or receiving treatment in a Washington Hospital," lay within the grounds. On Decoration Day, a detachment of Federal troops, patrolling the area, made sure to march "directly over the mounds rather than between them."[442] When a group of Southern women attempted to lay flowers on the graves, they found themselves brutally interrupted by the officer commanding the detachment who "picked up the flowers, tossed them to the ground, and crushed them underfoot. When a crowd gathered, he shouted, "Damn you, get away from here . . . or I'll make you."[443] Such treatment in the first years following the war may well have caused Southern women's memorial associations to move their thinking beyond memorialization and toward national vindication of the Confederate cause.

Historian Karen L. Cox contends that not only did Southern ladies' memorial associations found the Lost Cause or the Confederate Tradition, but they also became the driving force behind vindication and celebration. They aimed not only for freedom of action in the South but for national forgiveness and recognition of the rightness of the Confederate cause.[444] Work on establishment of an official

---

[439]   Neff, *Honoring the Civil War Dead*, 54, 55, 59, 60, 61.

[440]   Blair, *Cities of the Dead*, 54.

[441]   Ibid., 61.

[442]   Blair, *Cities of the Dead*, 73,

[443]   Ibid.

[444]   Karen L. Cox, *Dixie's Daughters* (Gainesville: University Press of Florida, 2003), 2-5.

Confederate Memorial Day began immediately after war's end as women strove to dignify their dead and what they had fought for. Eventually, they arrived at two dates: "either April 26, the day of General Joseph E. Johnston's surrender; or May 10, the day General Thomas 'Stonewall' Jackson died."[445] Women shared commemoration activities with their men from 1865 through the 1880s but took over power for good with the formation of the United Daughters of the Confederacy (UDC) in 1892. The greatest symbolic indication of their new power came with the unveiling of the Lee monument in Richmond on May 29, 1890. The massive equestrian statue of the Confederacy's premier general had been the responsibility of the female-dominated Lee Monument Association since 1884 and was regarded as a triumph by Southerners. The event, witnessed by 150,000, tripled the attendance at the Jackson statue ceremony in 1876. One onlooker exclaimed that he "felt as though [he was] assisting at a combined funeral and resurrection."[446] Historian David Blight writes, "Twenty-five years after a massive civil war, the military leader and the heroic symbol of the side that lost now sat high astride his horse, looking northward on a nation soon to incorporate him into its own pantheon."[447]

The United Daughters of the Confederacy exerted great influence in Southern classrooms by overseeing the content and design of history textbooks and reading lists well into the twentieth century. In this way, they molded the minds of new generations, perpetuating Lost Cause myths. Though much diminished today, Cox comments that "the organization's early history remains important to understanding how the New South was created in the image of the old."[448] For the purposes of this study, the focus is on the male-dominated, Jubal Early—led Virginia coalition which controlled most of the South's literary output through the *Southern Society Historical Papers* and related publications through the 1880s.

The path to destruction of Hood's historical memory began with his final report written to Richmond in February 1865. In particular, he sharply criticized General Joe Johnston's conduct, claiming it led to great waste in men and material along with gradual demoralization of the troops. Johnston's consistent policy of strategic withdrawal, with its vain hope of luring Sherman into a trap, had worn the men down.[449] Hood declared that he "was placed in command under the most trying [of] circumstances."[450] He went on to state that "the army was enfeebled in

---

[445]   Ibid., 4.

[446]   Gaines M. Foster, *Ghosts of the Confederacy* (New York: Oxford University Press, 1987), 101-102.

[447]   David W. Blight, *Race and Reunion: The Civil War in American Memory* (Cambridge: Harvard University Press, 2001), 269.

[448]   Cox, *Dixie's Daughters*, 163.

[449]   OR: I: XXXIIX, III, 636.

[450]   Ibid.

number and in spirit by a long retreat and severe and apparently fruitless losses."[451] Here, "fruitless" refers to Johnston's seeming reluctance to fight a decisive battle or to defend Atlanta. By engaging in a fabian strategy of fighting withdrawal, Johnston had given up over one hundred miles of territory, and by finally crossing the Chattahoochee, he had sacrificed the last natural barrier between Georgia's capital and the enemy. Hood also noted that during Johnston's tenure, the army "had dwindled day by day in partial engagements and skirmishes."[452]

Some of Hood's comments are open to debate. For example, Johnston undoubtedly fought battles. The distinction, later made by Hood in his memoirs, however, is that Johnston failed to fight a *general* battle. His had instead been a series of delaying engagements. Writing, in the aftermath of total defeat at Nashville, Hood may well have felt bitter about being placed in such a position. To be sure, he had lobbied for command, thinking that the aggressive tactics he favored would serve the Confederacy better that those employed by Johnston. By February 1865, only two months before war's end, however, he must have felt at least a little sorry that he had been motivated to do so. He might have wondered how things would have turned out had Johnston been more aggressive while the army was in better condition. Hood's report elicited a threat of legal action from Johnston and more importantly motivated Johnston to write his memoirs. Historian Brian Miller writes that this event "serves as the onset of Hood's postwar memory construction."[453] In his memoirs, Johnston attacked Hood, but when Hood defended himself, Lost Cause Johnston supporters, such as former generals Cadmus Wilcox and James Chalmers, joined in with negative comments of their own. Hood largely fought this battle alone as few chose to risk their own reputations by going up against Southern Historical Society writers.

Following the war, Hood settled in New Orleans and began building himself a place in the postwar world. He concentrated on business and charitable works, involving wounded veterans, widows, and orphans funds. He also took part in early efforts by the Southern Historical Society, established in the Louisiana capital to help the South come to terms with its losses, serving most notably as vice-president of the Lee Monument Association in 1870. Hood also reestablished connection with his former command, the Texas brigade, attending its first reunion held at Houston in 1872. In sum, by involving himself with public works by acting as a constructive citizen, he rebuilt feelings of self-worth shattered by the war and established a positive reputation for himself in New Orleans.[454]

Hood took the bait represented by critical content in Johnston's book and quickly began work on one of his own. Miller writes that Johnston "made Hood the

---

[451]   Ibid.

[452]   OR: XXXIIX, III, 636.

[453]   Miller, *John Bell Hood*, 203.

[454]   Miller, *John Bell Hood*, 178-179.

scapegoat, ridiculed his military actions, and deflected any possible blame for his own failure at Atlanta."[455] General Johnston's writings proved dry and overtechnical and did not sell well. The work had critics. A reviewer for the *New Orleans Daily Picayune* observed that "there are hyenas in human form who stand ready to tear open the grave of the buried past and whet their insatiable appetites for revenge upon the slain heroes . . . and spit their venom on those who survive."[456] Had Hood been able to step back, ignore Johnston's ill-selling memoirs, and continue his charitable works, the controversy may well have died. Unfortunately, his own combative nature would not allow this.

The most profound shift came when the Southern Historical Society relocated to Richmond, Virginia, in 1873. Once there, radical Southern nationalists from the Old Dominion led by Jubal A. Early, built upon romanticized Lost Cause ideology and aimed to recreate the Old South. Most importantly for Hood, Early's group sought whipping boys for defeat. Residents of New Orleans complained that their Historical Society had been hijacked. Indeed, they could have further claimed that the newly managed Southern Historical Society failed to represent the entire South.

Early's Virginians elevated themselves and their own state. Virginius Dabney, a well-known author and journalist of the day crowed, "We, Virginians, modestly admit our superiority to citizens of all other American states."[457] Tennessee Historian Thomas Connelly writes that Lost Cause architects "sought the best of both worlds—to be sorrowful, reluctant lovers of the Union who were dragooned into the secessionist camp. At the same time, they claimed to be leaders of that war against the Old Flag."[458] In short, such people constituted perhaps the most egotistical and hypocritical group one could have the misfortune to encounter upon the road of life.

The Virginia coalition used the Lost Cause to ease the region through hard times by memorializing the Southern war effort. Among its central tenets, the battle of Gettysburg became the crucial turning point of the war, the "high-water mark of the Confederacy." Southerners argued that the Confederacy succumbed because it ran up not against superior civilization and military strength but to overwhelming numbers and an unfair industrial advantage. Convenient villains such as "Lee's old war horse," Lieutenant General James Longstreet, and John Bell Hood shared blame for the loss in Pennsylvania. Hood assumed guilt not only for Gettysburg but for Confederate defeat in the West. The Battle of Franklin became symbolic for his overall performance. Finally, according to the ideology, slavery did not cause the war

---

[455]   Ibid., 203.

[456]   *New Orleans Daily Picayune,* January 8, 1874, in Miller, *John Bell Hood,* 201.

[457]   Thomas L. Connelly and Barbara Bellows, *God and General Longstreet: The Lost Cause and the Southern Mind* (Baton Rouge: LSU Press, 1982), 39.

[458]   Ibid., 41.

which morphed instead into a righteous dispute over the "true interpretation" of the constitution, specifically the tenth amendment supporting state sovereignty.[459]

"Old Jube" and his Virginia cohorts controlled virtually all of the South's literary output from 1865 to 1876, the period known as Reconstruction. The most important Lost Cause organ consisted of a large collection of articles and writings and came to be known as the *Southern Historical Society Papers,* but other publications including *Confederate Veteran, Our Living and Our Dead,* and *Southern Bivouac* played important roles in reconstructing the history of the war. Authors exerted Herculean efforts to explain away defeat. Since Virginians controlled the information machine, a complimentary national stereotype emerged. It featured a "moonlight and magnolias" interpretation of plantation society: While gallant cavaliers galloped across the landscape, breathless belles awaited their return and contented slaves praised their masters' generosity.[460]

Lost Cause writers transformed Robert E. Lee from a dependable military leader into a Confederate deity symbolic of Southern virtue. They made it possible for him to progress from Southern hero to inclusion within the *national* pantheon of military leaders. There, he would stand among such legendary figures as George Washington and Andrew Jackson. Through skillful manipulation, the commander, who had been modest in life, became all that glittered in Southern chivalry after death. This process reached completion with the unveiling of a massive statue of the general in Richmond on May 29, 1890.

Though Lost Cause artists possessed the power to enhance reputations, they could also wreck them.[461] Casting about for support and eager to castigate Hood for his actions, Johnston sought out a loyal former subordinate, Benjamin Franklin Cheatham. Cheatham, who had named his son after General Joe, expressed willingness to help in this new campaign. Perhaps he should not have been so willing to assist in denigrating Hood. After all, Hood had possessed the opportunity to remove him from command following Spring Hill and Franklin but held back. On December 8 and 9, 1864, Hood wrote to Secretary of War James Seddon concerning his corps commander. His first message withdrew an earlier recommendation that Cheatham be promoted, while the second requested someone to replace him in command. In a third communication, however, he withdrew the removal, stating

[459]   Connelly, *God and General Longstreet,* 23-25; Thomas Connelly, *The Marble Man: Robert E. Lee and His Image in American Society* (Baton Rouge: LSU Press, 1977), 64; Karen L. Cox, *Dixie's Daughters: The United Daughters of the Confederacy and the Preservation of Confederate Culture* (Gainesville: Univ. Press of Florida, 2003), 4.

[460]   Gaines M. Foster, *Ghosts of the Confederacy: Defeat the Lost Cause and the Emergence of the New South* (New York: Oxford University Press, 1987), 6; Connelly and Bellows, *God and General Longstreet,* 21; Connelly, *The Marble Man,* 68.

[461]   David W. Blight, *Race and Reunion: The Civil War in American Memory* (Cambridge: The Belknap Press of Harvard University Press, 2001), 267.

that though General Cheatham had made mistakes, he felt he could learn from them and should remain in command of his troops. In the immediate wake of events in Tennessee, Cheatham should have understood his mistakes and realized others did as well. Perhaps in the postwar years, especially with Lost Cause advocates seeking out scapegoats, Cheatham may have calculated in supporting Johnston, the Virginian, over Hood. After all, the Virginia coalition had momentum on its side and must have looked like a winning combination. In heaping blame on men like Longstreet and Hood, Cheatham, Johnston, Early, and others could exorcise their own demons—transferring their own guilt onto others.[462]

Hood's memoirs directly contradicted the creators of the Lost Cause myth which sought to glorify Virginians like Lee and Johnston and vilify men like Longstreet and Hood. In other words, Hood's accounting did not fit "within the collective memory being constructed across the South."[463] Though he would have preferred to leave his story to the "unbiased historians of the future," Hood felt that those writers would be unable to do him justice as Johnston had already prejudiced his case.[464]

In *Advance and Retreat*, Hood listed the reasons for failure in Tennessee: "The unfortunate affair at Spring Hill, the short duration of daylight at Franklin, and finally . . . [the] non-arrival of . . . expected reinforcements from the Trans-Mississippi Department."[465] He also offered a harsh assessment of General Johnston and asked, "Since [he] fought not a single *general* battle during the entire war of Secession, what just claim has he to generalship?" He further insisted that "had General Johnston possessed the requisite spirit and boldness to seize . . . various chances for victory, which were offered to him, he never would have allowed . . . Sherman to push him back one hundred miles in sixty-six days into the very heart of the Confederacy."[466]Hood concluded that though he "was not perfect, he certainly was no Joe Johnston."[467]

Hood's case was hurt by his untimely death from yellow fever in 1879. At that time, his memoir remained unpublished. General Beauregard took on that responsibility as part of an effort to raise money for the Hood orphan fund. *Advance and Retreat* gives a strong impression of being incomplete and looks like a rough draft. It appears that Hood became distracted by Johnston's ravings which caused him to meander away from his main purpose (to write a cogent memoir) and instead write a chapter entitled "Reply to General Johnston" which takes up eighty pages and turns his book into a polemic. Though much of the well-researched information contained in this chapter could have been useful if employed in other areas, the

---

[462] OR: I: XLV: III, 659 and 665. Miller, *John Bell Hood*, 204.

[463] Miller, *John Bell Hood*, 205.

[464] Ibid.

[465] Hood, *Advance and Retreat*, 304.

[466] Ibid., 316.

[467] Miller, *John Bell Hood*, 208.

argument with Johnston had no place within the book. Hood could have instead used his memoir as a platform to explain his experiences and actions. In this way, he could have answered much of the criticism directed against him and preempted much of what came in the future. *Advance and Retreat* would also have become a valuable historical document. As it stands, it is frustratingly incomplete. We have no way of knowing whether or not Hood would have chosen or been advised to rewrite what he had done.

Some modern historians now tend to side with Hood, at least in saying that opportunities existed for Johnston to seriously wound Sherman's army and greatly delay its advance into Georgia. Had Johnston attacked Sherman's vulnerable supply line with more determination, for example, he may have postponed the conquest of Atlanta until after the crucial 1864 United States presidential election. Basically, the strategy of attack on Sherman's railroad came down to an argument between Johnston, Jefferson Davis, and Braxton Bragg. The latter two contended that Johnston had sufficient cavalry to accomplish the task rather than employing Nathan Bedford Forrest's horsemen who busied themselves turning back Sherman's raids into Mississippi which Johnston wanted. "This impasse continued all through the remaining weeks of Johnston's command. As with the winter discussion of strategy for 1864, Johnston in Georgia and Davis in Richmond were unwilling or unable to trust each other. Nothing was decided on; nothing was resolved; nothing was done."[468] Historian Richard McMurry writes that sometime toward the end of May, Joe Johnston came to believe that despite his inability to halt Sherman's advance that "appearances to the contrary—his efforts had been a great strategic success."[469] A great part of this delusional optimism came from grossly overestimating Sherman's losses. For example, Johnston's chief of staff wrote glowingly on May 30 that "we have thus far succeeded in making . . . [Sherman] pay three of four [casualties] for every one of ours . . . , if we can keep this up, we win."[470]

Lost Cause artists who strove to stigmatize Hood ignored or minimized realities such as the above. The more Hood wrote in reply to Johnston's criticisms, the more they responded in kind toward him. Unfortunately for Hood, his memoirs were not published until after his death. At the end of a steamy New Orleans summer, General Hood fought his last battle, this time against yellow fever following his wife Anna-Marie and eldest daughter Lydia to the grave on August 27, 1879. His last wish had been that the Texas Brigade veterans take care of his ten orphaned children. Following his wife's passing on the twenty-fourth, members of his old brigade had

[468] Richard McMurry, *Atlanta 1864: The Last Chance for the Confederacy* (Lincoln: University of Nebraska Press, 1992), 98-99.
[469] Ibid., 96.
[470] Ibid.

written to him, stating in conclusion that though "the pall of sadness has fallen on you and yours, your old comrades share your poignant grief."[471]

The ever critical Southern Historical Society compressed its obituary of General Hood into a few words: "The death of General John B. Hood . . . is announced just as we are going to press, and we have only space to say that another gallant soldier, true patriot and highly atoned gentleman, has fallen at the post of duty."[472] Though Jubal Early gave a brief speech in Hood's memory in November of that year, it is notable that his words did not appear within the papers.

In striking contrast, national newspapers displayed more sympathy and recounted Hood's career in greater detail. The *Chicago Tribune* stated, "At dawn this morning, Gen. John B. Hood, the distinguished Confederate Chieftain, breathed his last . . . . Gen. Hood's malady was the result of over-anxiety and care, watching at the bedside of his devoted wife. He truly dies of a broken heart."[473] Though the *New York Herald* often echoed critical voices, it also stated that "Hood's thorough knowledge of the 'trade of war' and his force of character . . . courtesy and judgment . . . impressed officers and men alike with a sense of his fitness for command."[474] Closer to home, scribes wrote in ever more complimentary terms. The *New Orleans Times* commented, "It has been said . . . that he led his men into appalling perils, but . . . it must [also] be remembered that it was his fortune to participate in battles that were essentially desperate and that the humblest of his soldiers was never asked to go where he could not see his general also."[475] The writer concluded by stating that following the war Hood had developed into a "good citizen [and] honorable businessman."[476]

The most complimentary analysis came from New Orleans's largest paper, the *Daily Picayune*. Its writer not only stated that Hood would "always rank among the bravest and most chivalric of . . . Confederate leaders" but directly addressed controversy about his appointment to command the Army of Tennessee by affirming "Hood's splendid field record was eminently that of a fighting general," and in a swipe at Joe Johnston, "that was what the department deemed was needed—fighting." The *Picayune's* writer finished with a fine tribute to the general's memory. "Hood," it stated, "was known to everyone in this city and by everyone respected and admired." He had a "quite dignified manner," an "amiable expression of countenance," a "genial disposition," and a "well-informed mind." Underlining all of this praise,

[471] Miller, *John Bell Hood*, 220.

[472] *Southern Historical Society Papers*, ed. J. William Jones. Vol. 7 (Richmond, VA: Southern Historical Society, 1879), 496 and 585, in Miller, *John Bell Hood*, 225.

[473] *Chicago Tribune*, August 31, 1879, in Miller, *John Bell Hood*, 222.

[474] *New York Herald*, August 31, 1879, in Miller, *John Bell Hood*, 222.

[475] *New Orleans Times*, August 31, 1879, in Miller, *John Bell Hood*, 223.

[476] Ibid.

the obituary declared that "the very soul of honor and knighthood lived in that shattered frame."[477]

In contrast, Southern Historical Society writers assailed Hood after death for contributing to Confederate defeat. As previously mentioned (according to the Lost Cause), Gettysburg stood as the "high-water mark" for the South. Following that battle, so it was argued, Confederate fortunes had nowhere to go but down. Miller writes that "Hood's role at Gettysburg dominated conversation for several decades following the war."[478] Hood had favored a turning movement *around* Little Round Top, rather than a direct assault, which he thought would prove successful in routing the Union position and less costly in terms of casualties. General C. M. Wilcox felt convinced that Hood's three "inquiries about a change of attack delayed the entire advance of the Confederate force." In other words, Wilcox blamed the attack's ultimate failure on Hood, and his analysis appeared in the *Southern Historical Society Papers* in 1878. In truth, Hood's questioning of Lee's orders formed only a small part of much larger problems encountered on that hot July afternoon.[479]

The most outrageous claim blamed Hood for Sherman's March to the Sea. Following the fall of Atlanta, Hood withdrew from Georgia to Tennessee with the aim of taking Nashville. Ignoring the fact that plans for the Tennessee campaign had been developed by President Davis, Bragg, Beauregard, and Hood, the society chose to stigmatize Hood alone, insisting that "the movement of General Hood, ill-advised and pregnant with disaster, left the state of Georgia fairly open to a Federal advance."[480] This analysis also ignored the very real possibility of Confederate success had Hood been able to reach the Tennessee capital sooner than he did. It is also an "analysis" carried out largely with the aid of historical hindsight, a full knowledge of how badly things turned out rather than taking into account the Confederacy's precarious position and hopes for success at the time.

If someone should be "blamed" for the March to the Sea, it should rightly be Sherman. After all, it had been his responsibility, given by General Grant, to corner and destroy the Army of Tennessee. As we know, Sherman chose not to follow these orders. He tired of the chase, petitioned Grant to be allowed to march on Savannah, and left Thomas in charge of affairs in the Volunteer State. Moreover, using our own historical hindsight, we can see that Hood had almost no chance of defeating Sherman's great army in 1864 or any other year. Furthermore, Kennesaw Mountain

---

[477] *New Orleans Daily Picayune*, August 31, 1879 Morning edition, in Miller, *John Bell Hood*, 223.

[478] Miller, *John Bell Hood*, 212.

[479] *Southern Historical Society Papers*, Volume 6 (1878), 104 and 114-115, in Miller, *John Bell Hood*, 212.

[480] Miller, *John Bell Hood*, 212-213, *Southern Historical Society Papers*, Vol. 12 (1884): 298-299.

historian Dennis Kelly remarks that "even if the South had Alexander the Great and Napoleon Bonaparte, it would not have been able to stop Sherman."[481]

In the process of denigrating Hood, Southern Historical Society writers also improved the reputations of favored Confederate commanders such as Forrest. With Hood safely in his grave, former Army of Tennessee cavalry General James Chalmers claimed that had Forrest been in command at Spring Hill instead of Hood, Schofield would never have gotten away. As detailed in chapter 3, however, on the night of November 29, Hood specifically asked Forrest to block the Franklin Pike, but for various reasons, he failed to do so. Instead, he spewed forth "volumes" of impotent wrath at Confederate failures the following morning. How well would Forrest have done commanding a full army? Since his best previous experience was at cavalry corps level, we will never know. Similar questions have been raised in a somewhat different context about Stonewall Jackson. Forrest may not have been any better equipped for the additional responsibility than John Bell Hood. To argue otherwise is simply to engage in counterfactual debate.[482]

Miller writes that as late as 1959, the Southern Historical Society published remarks from the *Confederate Congressional Record* from 1865, employing Hood as whipping boy for failures by Joe Johnston. Tennessee Congressman Henry Foote complained bitterly that "the Army of Tennessee had been rudely deprived of its noble and gallant leader, General Johnston" and that since Hood had taken command, "there had been nothing in that quarter but an avalanche of misfortune." What Foote failed to mention, however, is that by this time in the war, the Confederacy as a whole was experiencing an "avalanche of misfortune." Whoever had command in the West would wind up as a scapegoat, regardless of their previous accomplishments. By inserting this critique among its writings, the Southern Historical Society thus managed to stain "Hood's reputation in the *Confederate Congressional record*."[483]

The Southern Historical Society constructed a blue print for General Hood, plumbed by historians, particularly from 1940 onward. Three writers from Tennessee stand out as particularly dominant: Stanley F. Horn, Thomas L. Connelly, and James Lee McDonough. Wiley Sword, though not a Tennessean, joined this group of anti-Hood scribes in 1992 with publication of *The Confederacy's Last Hurrah*. In recent years, Hood has experienced something of a renaissance with writers such as Richard McMurry, Russell Bonds, and Stephen Davis taking a more nuanced view.

---

[481]   Stephen Davis, "A Reappraisal of the Generalship of John Bell Hood in the Battles for Atlanta" in *The Campaign for Atlanta and Sherman's March to the Sea: Essays of the 1864 Georgia Campaigns*, Volume. I, eds. Theodore P. Salvas and David A. Woodbury (Campbell, CA: Savas-Woodbury Publishers, 1992), 82.

[482]   *Southern Historical Society Papers*, Vol. 7 (1879), 482, in Miller, *John Bell Hood*, 213.

[483]   *Southern Historical Society Papers*, ed. Frank Vandiver, Vol. 52 (Richmond, VA: Southern Historical Society, 1959), 21 and 283), in Miller, *John Bell Hood*, 213.

An important question is: Was the Lost Cause—promoted derisive image of the general universal in the immediate postwar years?

After time spent in Texas during the 1850s and experience with the men of the Texas Brigade, Hood wanted make his home in the Lone Star state following the war. Financial realities, however, dictated otherwise. He did visit Texas and the men of his old command several times primarily to take part in veteran activities. The *San Antonio Herald* stated on one such occasion, "It does our heart good to welcome back . . . , after an absence of over four years, this truly great and gallant officer, soldier, and gentleman. His history is well known to our readers." The writer noted sympathetically that Hood's "manly form has been hacked and pierced until it is now shorn of some of it fair proportions." Despite this, the correspondent remarked, "The general is in fine spirits and the full enjoyment of his health."[484]

The Texas Brigade, with Hood as its leader, stands out as unique among combat units. When General Lee needed decisive action to tip the scales of battle, Hood's men were employed as shock troops. Examples include Eltham's Landing, Gaines Mill, Second Manassas, and Gettysburg. After riding over the ground upon which the Texans made their attack at Gaines Mill, "Stonewall" Jackson exclaimed, "These men are soldiers indeed!" This came as high praise from Jackson, known to be sparing in his compliments.[485] Historian Harold B. Simpson writes that "the Hood-Texas brigade combination . . . was a great fighting machine, one of the best produced in America."[486] Moreover, McMurry remarks that "Hood led the brigade . . . [in] a series of engagements that won for it a reputation unmatched in Civil War annals."[487] The men felt a particular affection for their commander. Infantryman Tine Owen of the 4th Texas regiment (Hood's first command), for example, reacted with disappointment to news that his new baby brother had been named "William Travis" instead of "John Hood."[488]

The Texas Brigade Association, established in 1872, aimed to preserve the memory of its general and men. Though active in group affairs, Hood found himself restricted by financial and health concerns to attending only two reunions. At the first, held in 1872, many veterans saw their old leader for the first time since Chickamauga. There Hood found himself "greeted with great enthusiasm . . . [and] called to the chair by acclamation."[489] At Hood's final reunion in 1877 held

---

[484]   *San Antonio Herald* article reprinted in the *New Orleans Daily Picayune*, July 22, 1865, in Miller, *John Bell Hood*, 176.

[485]   (Douglas Southall Freeman, *Lee's Lieutenants*. Volume I (New York: Charles Scribner's Sons, 1942), 535)

[486]   Harold B. Simpson, *Hood's Texas Brigade, Vol. I* (Fort Worth: Landmark Publishing, Inc., 1999) 90.

[487]   Polley, *Hood's Texas Brigade*, Introduction.

[488]   Taken from Owen Letters, March 15, 1862, in Simpson, *Hood's Texas Brigade*, 91.

[489]   Simpson, *Hood's Texas Brigade*, Vol. II, 158.

in Waco, the general found his speech "constantly interrupted by the cheers of old comrades" and "heavy applause."[490] One month prior to Hood's death on July 9, 1879, members at the reunion held in Palestine, Texas, passed a resolution guaranteeing him a free railroad pass "to and from all . . . reunions for the rest of his life."[491] Simpson comments that heavy financial losses had left Hood in dire circumstances, not helped by the yellow fever epidemic that struck New Orleans that year, and that these circumstances motivated the association's resolution. Following Hood's death, at a special meeting on September 13 held in Houston, members put forth plans to offer help to the Hood orphans. In the end, the Texas Brigade Association involved itself in the welfare of their late general's children for twenty years.[492] The 1887 reunion held at Austin displayed dramatic evidence of enduring affection for General Hood. One speaker, Major Howdy Martin, after thrilling his audience with an account of Texan exploits at Gettysburg where Hood had been severely wounded, displayed the general's frock coat whose "bloodstains and . . . missing sleeve [gave] mute evidence to . . . sacrifice offered." Overcome with emotion, the old soldiers crowded around the speaker's platform, many with tears in their eyes and "sacredly touched the garment, some even kissing it and clasping it to their breasts."[493]

Joe Johnston's memoirs had been in circulation since 1873, and Lost Cause architects had been chipping away at Hood's reputation almost from the end of the war, yet this made no difference to Texans who had fought under Hood. These men had seen greater casualty rates than those suffered by the Army of Tennessee, including Gaines Mill, where losses stood at forty-percent or more. That battle included a frontal assault on fortified enemy positions, yet it represented definitive victory and had been ordered by General Lee. The Texas Brigade fought with Hood at a time when Confederate hopes had been high. Gaines Mill represented one of a series of battles that drove Unionists out of Virginia. Tennessee, on the other hand, stood for the funereal stage of the Confederacy's existence. The men of Texas remembered their battles differently than did those who marched through the drenching Tennessee winter of 1864. In short, anyone who had been in command at that time, even Joe Johnston, would likely have been made a scapegoat.

Richmond Examiner editor and Lost Cause historian E. A. Pollard wrote that Hood had "a lion's heart and a wooden head." Other Southern Historical Society writers alleged that Army of Tennessee soldiers commonly referred to their general

---

[490] Taken from the Waco *Daily Examiner*, June 28, 1877, in Simpson, *Hood's Texas Brigade*, Vol. II, 160.
[491] Taken from the Brigade association minute book, 45, in Simpson, *Hood's Texas Brigade*, Vol. II, 161.
[492] Simpson, *Hood's Texas Brigade*, Vol. II, 161-162.
[493] Ibid., 169.

as "Old Woodenhead."[494] Applying the "Woodenhead" label made it easy to imply that John Bell Hood was stupid. Implications about Hood's intelligence "appear to be retrospective," originating from a campaign led by postwar Lost Cause and pro-Johnston partisans . . . ."[495] From such techniques, one does not need to travel far to find Wiley Sword's *The Confederacy's Last Hurrah*. Clearly, "historians" of the Jubal Early school wanted Hood to be not only *the* scapegoat for Confederate disaster in the West but a stupid man as well. This is often the portrait painted by modern historians, especially Horn, Connelly, Sword, and McDonough. The Lost Cause dominated. It continues to influence historical output concerning the Civil War and has assigned specific roles to actors in America's great national tragedy.

---

[494]   Bonds, *War Like a Thunderbolt*, 77. Bonds indicate that he has found no contemporaneous letter or diary accounts that prove this true. Instead nicknames for the Kentuckian included simply "Hood," "The Sergeant" because of his loud voice and commanding demeanor, and "Old Pegleg." It seems that nearly all Civil War generals were referred to as "Old" even if only in their early thirties. For example, James Longstreet acquired the nickname of "Old Peter," and classmates of George Thomas referred to him as "Old Tom" while students at West Point.

[495]   Ibid.

CHAPTER 7

Conclusion

The historical roles that Civil War actors would play became clear in the years following the conflict. In many cases, a funeral of each man's life reflected his place within the hierarchy of wartime leadership. Sometimes this occurred by design and sometimes because of the circumstances in their lives. General Thomas, because of his solid performance and pivotal role in northern victory, and Robert E. Lee, because of his recognized position as premier general of the Confederacy, passed from life with suitably dignified ceremony and national publicity. General Hood's end-of-life observances, however, possessed a more muted character. By the time of his death in 1879, the Kentuckian had been firmly saddled with the mantle of scapegoat not only for Gettysburg but also for Southern defeat in the West. Much to the talent of Lost Cause architects, the last act of his dramatic life was overshadowed by poverty and a severe yellow fever epidemic. Hood left the stage in quiet obscurity.

On the rainy morning of March 28, 1870, General George Thomas sat down in his San Francisco office to answer a curious and outrageous letter which had appeared in the *New York Tribune* on March 12. Thomas had come to be in San Francisco as commander of the Pacific Division by order of President Grant in 1869. The *Tribune* letter, signed anonymously by "one who fought at Nashville," asserted that not only had Grant's retraction of his order placing Schofield in command been "a blunder," but also that Thomas had been too slow. Furthermore, the writer maintained that the battle had actually been won at Franklin two weeks earlier, where "the enemy had been whipped until there was very little in him."[496] On March 19, another letter had appeared, this time defending Thomas, and signed, "Another man who fought at Nashville." Its author noted that Schofield had been successful by accident, not by design, at Franklin; but he also remarked that "so well was [the Nashville strategy] planned and so scientifically and thoroughly was the plan carried out, that to-day it is made a study at the military academy among the great battles

---

[496]   General Jacob Cox, *New York Tribune*, March 12, 1870, in Frank A. Palumbo, *The Dependable General* (Dayton, Ohio: Morningside House, Inc., 1983), 388.

of history." The writer concluded that "nobody who knows what that army was, and what its failings were, will dare to dispute the fact that Thomas' removal would have proved a great, if not fatal error."[497]

As it turned out, the original letter had been written by General Jacob Cox, one of Schofield's corps commanders, and if not instigated by, at least had the approval of his former boss. It seems that Schofield had become piqued by the fact that Grant's original order placing him in command at Nashville was now publicly regarded as a mistake. In effect, the *Tribune* letter, as General David Stanley later asserted, aimed for revenge. Bobrick writes that Grant may have been involved. Cox was a member of his cabinet. "Thomas's formidable name had just been floated . . . as a presidential candidate, and some think Grant and his political allies had moved at once to tarnish his image and preemptively sweep him from the scene."[498] If true, the warriors turned politicians had nothing to fear. Like Sherman, Thomas had absolutely no desire to be president.

Thomas, worn out by the war and upset over this aggressive assault on his reputation, suffered a fatal stroke while writing his reply. The government almost immediately went into high gear planning the funeral of one of its great commanders. Though Sherman wanted Thomas buried at West Point, Thomas's wife demurred, stating her wish that the general rest in her family's private plot in Troy, New York. That Mrs. Thomas should resist government-sponsored effort to honor her husband is significant. She had long felt that Grant tried to humiliate Thomas. She stated that the president's behavior had "preyed upon and affected his health" and that "Schofield's base attack on his military reputation" added to the pain and "was the cause of the fatal attack on March 28, 1870."[499] The government did provide a special train to take Thomas's body from the Pacific coast to New York. The start of the general's final journey is poignant. McKinney writes,

> At 6:30 a.m. on March 30, the coffin was put aboard the Oakland ferry and, as the little steamer left the San Francisco dock, the first of fifty-four-minute guns [one for each year of his life] sounded from the fort on Alcatraz Island. Anchored in the stream, her hull hidden by the fog drifting through the Golden Gate, Her Britannic Majesty's frigate *Zealous* answered Alcatraz gun for gun. At Oakland Point, the coffin was placed in a special car and at 8:00 a.m. started for Troy, New York.[500]

---

[497]   Ibid., 389.

[498]   Bobrick, *Master of War*, 329.

[499]   John N. Hough papers, quoted in Coupee, *Thomas*, 617, in Bobrick, *Master of War*, 332. Colonel Hough who served with Thomas in Tennessee, was his aide while in San Francisco, and helped organize the family papers after the general's death.

[500]   McKinney, *Education in Violence*, 471-472.

Mrs. Thomas did allow Sherman to organize a military funeral attended by President Grant. The parade from church to cemetery extended over one mile in length as people paid tribute.[501]

But what of Thomas's place in history? That he had been one of the war's most able commanders stood without doubt, yet how high would his position be? General Joseph Hooker who commanded the XX corps as part of the Army of the Cumberland named him "the ablest, most just, and the most beloved man I ever knew. I shall never know his equal. I never supposed a man of his merit could live."[502] General Henry Boynton commented, "Of him and him alone can it be truthfully said that he never lost a movement or a battle."[503] General James Steedman praised him most, calling Thomas "the grandest character of the war, the noblest figure of the Great Rebellion, the most accomplished soldier America ever produced."[504]

During the 1880s and 1890s, a clique of four men did all they could to control northern Civil War memory: Grant, Sherman, Sheridan, and Schofield.[505] Each rose to a position of great political or military power; Grant as president, Sherman as general-in-chief, Schofield as Secretary of War, and Sheridan as general-in-chief. All worked together to ensure their own high place in American history, sometimes accomplished at the expense of others. "Gamaliel Bradford noted in *Union Portraits*," for example, that "Grant was apt to couple Thomas's name with some innuendo as was Sherman . . . ."[506] The most lasting word associated with Thomas, thanks to both Grant and Sherman, is "slow." Grant also stated in his memoir, taking aim at Nashville, "He was not as good . . . in pursuit as in action."[507] Because of their great stature, the opinions of men like Grant and Sherman cannot and have not been taken lightly. Civil War historians have thus come to accept a view of Thomas as a solid, dependable commander who at times could be slow and needed prodding from superiors such as Grant and Sherman. Noted historian Bruce Catton writes, "Thomas comes down in history as the Rock of Chickamauga, the great defensive fighter, the man who could never be driven away . . . . That may be a correct appraisal. Yet it may also be worth making note that just twice in the war was a major Confederate army driven away from a prepared position in complete route—at Chattanooga and Nashville. Each

[501] Ibid., 473.

[502] Society of the Army of the Cumberland, *Yearbook*, 1871, 71 in Bobrick, *Master of War,* 333.

[503] Piatt and Boynton, *Thomas*, 76-77, in Bobrick, *Master of War,* 334.

[504] "Talk with General Steedman," in the *New York Times*, Nov. 24, 1879, in Bobrick, *Master of War,* 334.

[505] Bobrick, *Master of War,* 334.

[506] Gamaliel Bradford, *Union Portraits* (Boston: Houghton Mifflin, 1916),130, in Bobrick, *Master of War,* 335.

[507] Grant Memoirs in Bobrick, *Master of War,* 624.

time, the blow that routed it was launched by Thomas."[508] Catton later admitted to having a "haunting feeling" that Thomas may have been "the best [general] of them all." He went on to muse that history would need to be "upgraded" for him to have his proper place and concluded that "there was nothing slow about Thomas . . . or "primarily defensive . . . Grant was wrong."[509]

That same year in the South, Robert E. Lee died on October 12. He had been serving as president of Washington College, now Washington and Lee. Cadets from the nearby Virginia Military Institute (VMI) filled an important role in the funeral ceremonies, guarding the general's body the night before. One of the young men selected for that honorable duty, William Nalle, wrote to his mother giving details of the sad event:

> All business was suspended . . . all over the country and town and all duties . . . suspended at the institute . . . all the black crepe and similar black material in Lexington was used up at once, and they had to send to Lynchburg for more. Every cadet had black crepe issued to him, and an order was published . . . requiring us to wear it as badge of mourning for six months.[510]

An account of the funeral in the *Lexington Gazette* dated October 21, 1870, described the congregation as "vast and impressive . . . [and remarked that] . . . the deepest solemnity pervaded the entire multitude." Here, we see testimony that Lee held a high position in Southern society even before reworking by Lost Cause strategists. A veteran recalled his general as "the grandest thing in all the world to us . . . we trusted him like a providence and obeyed him like a god."[511]

Nine years later, one of the South's most prominent generals, in contrast, received but an abbreviated ceremony. Only a few friends accompanied the wooden casket to Lafayette No.1 cemetery from Trinity Episcopal Church, while a local militia group provided a military touch. "The houses along the way were shuttered. The streets were empty. No one paid a moment's attention to another of yellow jack's thousands of victims."[512] No matter the cause of death, it seems clear General Hood had been selected by fate and circumstance to fill the role of scapegoat for

---

[508] Bruce Catton, *Hallowed Ground*, 283, in Bobrick, *Master of War*, 226.

[509] Bruce Catton, "Rock of Chickamauga," (Review of F. F. McKinney *Education in Violence*, http://home.earthlink.net/~oneplaz/majorgeneralgeorgehthomasblogsite/.

[510] www.vmi.edu/archiv Virginia Military Institute Archives, "The Funeral of General Robert E. Lee," 1-2. William Nalle letter, "The Funeral of General Robert E. Lee," March 4, 2011.

[511] "Funeral of General R. E. Lee," www.gdg.org/Research/People/RELEe, March 4, 2011.

[512] McMurry, *John Bell Hood*, 203; Richard O'Connor, *Hood: Cavalier General* (New York: Prentice-Hall, Inc., 1949), 278.

Southern defeat, or an effort would have been made to celebrate his passing in a more dignified way.

John Bell Hood had not been reckless, he had not been a borderline "psychotic" who "associated valor with casualty figures,"[513] and he certainly had not been stupid. His fate in the end appears driven by forces beyond his control. After experiencing great success with General Lee in the war's early years, he took command of the Confederacy's western army at a time when Southern fortunes rapidly reached their nadir. In short, he had chosen to ride the whirlwind, and it had defeated him.

In examining the postwar years and Hood's attempt to recreate a normal life for himself, one is struck by the irony of the Lost Cause. White Southern Confederates (Hood and Longstreet) who almost died in service of the Confederacy found themselves attacked by other white Southern Confederates constructing an ideology to glorify the Confederacy. Both men have been portrayed as betrayers, yet who are the real traitors? When the war ended, Hood worked to retrieve his lost manhood by doing good works. He found a home, a wife, children, and community respect in New Orleans. During that time, he encountered the Lost Cause and the men of the Virginia coalition who worked to assign him another role in history. He fought against this new enemy, striving to defend himself and tell the truth about his role until he died. Even after death, however, especially after death, the revisers of history kept at their work.

The Lost Cause is not a thing of the past; it is organic and has successfully adapted itself as the years have passed. Today, it continues to divide Americans by offering up a subversive version of Civil War history. As we begin to celebrate the Civil War Sesquicentennial, we find ourselves faced with the same issues brought forth in the 1870s and 1880s; slavery had nothing to do with the war, and Southerners fought heroically against insurmountable odds for principle, the idea that the Constitution guaranteed states the right to secede. A disturbing number of people continue to believe these myths, and interestingly, they seem, at least generally, to be separated along blue state-red state lines.

On April 24, 2011, the *CBS Sunday Morning* show had as a section of its program, a short segment on the Civil War Sesquicentennial. The host introduced the program, noting that disagreements about causes for the war are still lively. One female Union Civil War reenactor, a school teacher in everyday life, remarked that a stigma is often attached to reenactors of the Civil War; one not applied to living history presenters of the Revolutionary War or any other conflict. There seems, she noted, to be widespread belief that they want to restart the conflict to fight it over again in real terms. Bernard Powers, a professor of African-American history at the College of Charleston, paraphrased William Faulkner, commenting that in the South, the "past is not dead; it's not even over." He stated that though today's America is much different than that of 1961 when the Centennial was celebrated, many old beliefs

---

[513]   Connelly, *The Army of Tennessee*, 431.

persist. Nicole Green, director of the Old Slave Mart museum in Charleston, said that few visitors seek the *Gone with the Wind*, hoop skirt, mint julep story anymore." She felt that today, people search for deeper meanings. In contrast, venerable June Wells, past national president of the United Daughters of the Confederacy and head docent at the Charleston Confederate Museum, expressed unrestrained pride in her Confederate heritage. Perhaps most importantly, the program featured a new poll produced by the Pew Research Center which reveals that while 38 percent of Americans believe the war to have been about slavery, another 48 percent attribute its cause to "states rights." Does this indicate that the Lost Cause is winning the war for memory?[514]

Historian David Blight locates several indicators that this may be so in his essay, "The Theft of Lincoln in Scholarship, Politics, and Public Memory."[515] Both the far left and the far right have molded Lincoln to fit their own agendas. Lerone Bennett claims that the president's supporters have turned "a racist who wanted to deport all blacks into a symbol of integration and brotherhood."[516] That is the militant, left-wing, black history version. More troubling is what comes from the other side. Charles Adams in *When in the Course of Human Events: Arguing the Case for Southern Secession* (2000) compares Lincoln's ruthlessness in prosecuting a war with unconditional surrender to that of Stalin and Hitler in World War II. Adams considers Lincoln a virulent racist and calls the second inaugural "Psychopathic," a mere cover for his larger motive, the destruction of Southern civilization. During Reconstruction, according to Adams, the Union Leagues were the terrorist wing of the Republican Party and the Ku Klux Klan a harmless, necessary veterans' organization.[517]

Thomas J. Di Lorenzo, in *The Real Lincoln: A New Look at Abraham Lincoln, His Agenda, and an Unnecessary War* (2002), argues that Lincoln was "the godfather of big government." For Di Lorenzo, "leaders of secession were the Civil War's real heroes . . . because their cause had nothing to do with slavery—only with resisting federal tyranny." He regards the Fourteenth and Fifteenth Amendments as nothing more than "huge extensions of federal power."[518] Both writers are virulent Lincoln-haters and Confederate apologists. Blight asks, "Why pay attention to these books?" His answer is that they sell better than more scholarly, well-researched works by authors such as James McPherson, Eric Foner, and others.

---

[514] CBS Sunday Morning Show, April 24, 2011.

[515] In Eric Foner, ed., *Our Lincoln: New Perspectives on Lincoln and His World* (New York: W. W. Norton, 2008), Chapter 11.

[516] Lerone Bennett, *Forced into Glory: Abraham Lincoln's White Dream* (Chicago, 2000) in Blight, *Our Lincoln*, 274.

[517] Blight, *Our Lincoln*, 276.

[518] Ibid., 277.

The Ken Burns Civil War series, rebroadcast for the Sesquicentennial in April of this year, has been the most popular program ever aired on PBS. In its first production in September 1990, forty million Americans watched in fascination. The film was remastered in 2002 to bring it up to date with current technology. During this time, minor errors, such as getting Lincoln's age at death wrong were corrected, but to this writer's knowledge, no major changes have been made in the film's content. Probably, the series' greatest accomplishment lies in how it stimulated public interest in the Civil War. This aside, however, Burn's production has problems. Military historian Gary Gallagher contends that it employs,

> An old-fashioned geographical imbalance between the eastern and western theaters of the war stressed Gettysburg at the expense of many other neglected turning points . . . and served up a thoroughly traditional profile of Robert E. Lee as a military genius, never recognizing the vigorous debate over the years about his ideas and generalship.[519]

Perhaps the most important point recognized by Gallagher is that Burns actually fed Lost Cause mythology not only by overemphasizing Gettysburg but also by bestowing upon the Confederacy a "mantle of hopelessness." From the very beginning, Burns supported one of the main tenets of the Lost Cause that the South never had a chance to win and fought nobly against "overwhelming numbers and resources."[520]

Columbia University historian Eric Foner rightly criticized the film's final episode, finding it "profoundly disturbing" that after spending so much time on battles, personalities, and other details, it gave only slight attention to Reconstruction and the "long-term consequences of the conflict." Instead, Burns fast forwarded to aged veterans shaking hands across the stone wall at Gettysburg, the metaphorical "bloody chasm." The major problem recognized by Foner and historian Leon Litwack "is that the audience never learns how and why that reconciliation came about at what political and social costs sectional union triumphed while racial division only deepened."[521] The point here is that great as this film's contributions have been and twenty-one years after its first production, it still contains incomplete and in some areas, slanted history.

This paper's purpose has been to right historical wrongs done to Confederate General John Bell Hood to attempt to set the record straight regarding his military career and to overturn the "woodenhead" label. The purpose has also been to reveal how dominant individuals and groups have been able to influence the flow of

[519] David Blight, *Beyond the Battlefield: Race, Memory, and the American Civil War* (Amherst: University of Massachusetts Press, 2002), 215.

[520] Ibid.

[521] David Blight, *Beyond the Battlefield,* 215.

history. George Thomas had faith that one day, history would do him justice, and this wish has been largely fulfilled in recent years. One of the best Civil War magazines, *North & South*, for example, had an issue featuring an article entitled, "The Top Ten Generals." In it, Thomas was ranked fourth among all commanders blue and gray. One of the panel's historians even ranked him third, ahead of Sherman.[522] For Hood things are improving too but at a slower pace. Brian Miller's 2010 book provides the first truly balanced examination of the general's life. Biographies over the years, even those one might deem "sympathetic," however, have presented him as the South's romantic, reckless cavalier. There remains much to be done. The *Southern Historical Society Papers* contain a veritable gold mine for historians when it comes to men like Hood and Longstreet. Here lies a ready-made story about their careers which is still tempting to some writers. One hundred and fifty years following its conclusion, the complete story of the Civil War and its actors remains unfinished. Perhaps this will always be so, but the battle for historical objectivity will never be won without constant struggle. Historian Leopold Von Ranke once remarked that we must strive to write history as it really was, *wie es eigentlich gewesen ist.*[523] In practical terms, this is probably impossible; too many barriers stand between us and events of the past for absolute accuracy to be obtained. Historians, however, should *try* to do this, to get as close as they can. After all, it is this kind of effort that separates us from writers of fiction. The further back we stand from an event, the greater our perspective becomes. History, like a well-kept garden, requires regular maintenance; the weeds must be removed so that flowers can be seen at their best advantage. Put another way, as Civil War historian Bruce Catton once observed, there are times when history needs upgrading.[524]

---

[522] *North & South* magazine, Vol. 6, number 4.

[523] Bjanepr.Wordpress.com

[524] Bruce Catton, "Rock of Chickamauga," http://home.earthlink.net/~oneplaz/majorgeneral eorgehthomasblogsite/.)

BIBLIOGRAPHY

Primary Sources:

Alexander, E. P. *Memoirs of a Confederate.* Da Capo Press, 1993 (No city of publication is given.)

Brown, Norman, ed. *One of Cleburne's Command: The Civil War Reminiscences and Diary of Captain Samuel T. Foster, Greenburg's Texas Brigade CSA.* Austin: University of Texas Press, 1980.

Chesnut, Mary. *A Diary from Dixie.* Boston: Houghton Mifflin, 1949.

Cozzens, Peter and Robert I. Girardi, eds. *The New Annals of the Civil War.* Mechanicsburg, PA, Stackpole Books, 2004.

Dowdey, Clifford and Louis H. Manarin, eds. *The Wartime Papers of R. E. Lee.* New York: Bramhall House, 1941.

Fremantle, Lieutenant Colonel Arthur J. L. *Three Months in the Southern States-April to June 1863.* Lincoln: University of Nebraska Press, 1991.

Gibbon, John, *The Artillerist's Manual.* Dayton: Morningside Press, 1991.

Grant, U. S., *Personal Memoirs of U. S. Grant, Selected Letters 1839-1865.* New York: Literary Classics of the United States, Inc., 1990.

Hood, Lieutenant General J. B. *Advance and Retreat.* Edison, NJ: Blue and Grey Press, 1985.

Johnson, Robert Underwood and Clarence Clough Buell, eds. Battles and Leaders Series. Vol. 4. New York: The Century Company, 1884, 1888.

Logsdon, David R., ed. *Eyewitnesses at the Battle of Franklin.* Nashville: Kettle Mills Press, 2000.

McCann, William, ed. *Ambrose Bierce's Civil War.* "What Occurred at Franklin." New York: Wings Books, 1996.

Polley, J. B. *Hood's Texas Brigade.* Dayton Morningside Bookshop, 1998. Originally published as *A Soldiers Letters to Charming Nellie* in 1908.

Scofield, Levi T. *The Retreat from Pulaski to Nashville-Battle of Franklin, Tennessee, November 30, 1864.* Cleveland: Press of the Caxton Co., 1909.

Sherman, W. T. *Memoirs of General William T. Sherman, by Himself.* Vol. II. Bloomington: University of Indiana Press, 1957.

Simpson, John A., ed. *Reminiscences of the Forty-First Tennessee: The Civil War in the West.* Shippensburg: White Mane Books, 2001.

Van Horne, Thomas B. *History of the Army of the Cumberland.* Vol. II. Wilmington: Broadfoot Publishing Co. 1988. Originally entered into the Library of Congress in 1875.

War of the Rebellion: Records of the Union and Confederate Armies. 128 Vols. Washington: Governments Printing Office, 1886. (Series I)

Watkins, Sam. *Company Aytch.* New York: Penguin Putnam, 1989. Originally published in Nashville by Cumberland Presbyterian Publishing House in 1882. Watkins served in the Army of Tennessee.

Wilson, James H. *Under the Old Flag.* Vol. II. New York: D. Appleton, 1911.

Secondary Sources:

Blair, William, *Cities of the Dead: Contesting the Memory of the Civil War South, 1865-1914.* Chapel Hill: University of North Carolina Press, 2004.

Blight, David W. *Beyond the Battlefield: Race, Memory, and the American Civil War.* Amherst: University of Massachusetts Press, 2002.

Blight, David W. *Race and Reunion: The Civil War in American Memory.* Cambridge: The Belknap Press of Harvard University Press, 2001.

Bobrick, Benson. *Master of War: The Life of General George H. Thomas.* New York: Simon & Schuster, 2009.

Bonds, Russell S. *War Like the Thunderbolt: The Battle and Burning of Atlanta.* Yardley, PA: Westholme Publishing LLC, 2009.

Buell, Thomas B. *The Warrior Generals: Combat Leadership in the Civil War.* New York: Three Rivers Press, 1997.

Castel, Albert. *Decision in the West: The Atlanta Campaign of 1864.* University Press of Kansas, 1992.

Catton, Bruce. "Rock of Chickamauga," book review of F. F. McKinney's *Education in Violence.* http://home.earthlink.net/~oneplez/majorgeneralgeorgehthomasblogsite.

Connelly, Thomas L. *Autumn of Glory: The Army of Tennessee: 1862-1865.* Baton Rouge: LSU Press, 1971.

Connelly, Thomas L., and James Lee McDonough. *Five Tragic Hours: The Battle of Franklin.* Knoxville: University of Tennessee Press, 1983.

Connelly, Thomas L. and Barbara Bellows. *God and General Longstreet: The Lost Cause and the Southern Mind.* Baton Rouge: LSU Press, 1982.

Connelly, Thomas L. *The Marble Man: Robert E. Lee and His Image in American Society.* Baton Rouge: LSU Press, 1977.

Cox, Karen. *Dixie's Daughter's: The United Daughters of the Confederacy and Preservation of Confederate Culture.* Gainesville: University of Florida Press, 2003.

Davis, Stephen. *Atlanta Will Fall: Sherman, Joe Johnston, and the Yankee Heavy Battalions.* Wilmington: SR Books, 2001.

Dyer, John P. *The Gallant Hood.* Indianapolis: Bobbs Merrill Co., 1950.

Escott, Paul D. *After Secession: Jefferson Davis and the Failure of Confederate Nationalism.* Baton Rouge: LSU Press, 1978.

Faust, Drew Gilpin, *The Republic of Suffering: Death and the American Civil War.* New York: Alfred A. Knopf, 2008.

Freeman, Douglas Southall. *Lee's Lieutenants.* Vol. I. New York: Charles Scribner's Sons, 1942.

Furgurson, Ernest B. *Not War but Murder: Cold Harbor 1864*. New York: Alfred Knopf, 2000.

Foner, Eric, ed. *Our Lincoln: New Perspectives of Lincoln and His World*. New York: W. W. Norton, 2008.

Foster, Gaines M. *Ghosts of the Confederacy: Defeat, the Lost Cause, and the Emergence of the New South*. New York: Oxford University Press, 1987.

"Funeral of General Robert E. Lee." www.gdg.org/Research/People/RELEE

Gallagher, Gary W. *The American Civil War: Great Courses in Modern History*. Lecture Series, Part I. Chantilly, Va., Teaching Company, 2000.

Gallagher, Gary and Joseph T. Glatthar eds. *Leaders of the Lost cause: New Perspectives on the Confederate High Command*. Mechanicsburg: Stockpole Books, 2004.

Gallagher, Gary W. *Lee and His Generals in War and Memory*. Baton Rouge: LSU Press, 1998.

Gillum, Jamie. *The Battle of Spring Hill-Twenty Five Hours to Tragedy*. Copyright by James F. Gillum, 2004.

Groom, Winston. *Shrouds of Glory*. New York: Grove Press, 1995.

Hay, Thomas Robson. *Hood's Tennessee Campaign*. Dayton: Morningside Bookshop, 1976. Originally published in 1929 and awarded the Robert M. Johnston Military History Prize by the American Historical Association for 1920 as an essay.

Holy Bible-Concordance. Oxford: Oxford University Press.

Horn, Stanley F. *The Army of Tennessee*. Norman: University of Oklahoma Press, 1941.

Horn, Stanley F. *The Decisive Battle of Nashville*. Baton Rouge: LSU Press, 1956, 1984.

Jacobson, Eric and Richard A. Rupp. *For Cause & For Country: A Study of the Affair at Spring Hill and the Battle of Franklin*. Franklin: O'More Publishing, 2006.

Levine, Bruce. *Confederate Emancipation: Southern Plans to Free and Arm Slaves during the Civil War*. New York: Oxford, 2006.

McCusker, John J., and Russell R. Menard. *The Economy of British America, 1607-1789*. Chapel Hill: University of North Carolina Press, 1985.

McDonough, James Lee. *Stones River: Bloody Winter in Tennessee*. Knoxville: University of Tennessee Press, 1980.

McKinney, Francis F. *Education in Violence: The Life of General George H. Thomas and the History of the Army of the Cumberland*. Chicago: Americana House Inc., 1991.

McMurry, Richard. *Atlanta 1864: Last Chance for the Confederacy*. Lincoln: University of Nebraska, 2000.

McMurry, Richard M. "Confederate Morale in the Atlanta Campaign of 1864," *Georgia Historic Quarterly*, 54 (1970), 233.

McMurry, Richard. *John Bell Hood and the War for Southern Independence*. Lincoln: University of Nebraska Press, 1992.

McPherson, James M. *Battle Cry of Freedom*. New York: Oxford, 2003.

McWhiney, Grady and Perry Jamieson. *Attack and Die: Civil War Military Tactics and the Southern Heritage*. Tuscaloosa: University of Alabama Press, 1982.

Miller, Brian C. *John Bell Hood and the Fight for Civil War Memory*. Knoxville: University of Tennessee Press, 2010.

Neff, John R., *Honoring the Civil War Dead: Commemoration and the Problems of Reconciliation*. Lawrence: University Press of Kansas, 2005.

Nosworthy, Brent. *The Bloody Crucible of Courage: Fighting Methods and Combat Experience of the Civil War*. New York: Carroll and Graf Publishers, 2003.

O'Connor, Richard. *Hood: Cavalier General*. New York: Prentice Hall, Inc., 1949.

Potter, David M. *The Impending Crisis: 1848-1861*. New York: Harper and Row, 1976.

Rakove, Jack. *Revolutionaries: A New History of the Invention of America*. New York: Houghton Mifflin Harcourt, 2010.

Savas, Theodore P., and David A. Woodbury, eds. *The Campaign for Atlanta and Sherman's March to the Sea: Essays of the 1864 Campaigns*. Campbell, CA: Savas Woodbury Publishers, 1992.

Sayers, Althea. *The Sound of Brown's Guns: The Battle of Spring Hill, November 29, 1864.* Spring Hill: Rosewood Publishing, 1995.

Schantz, Mark S., *Awaiting the Heavenly Country.* Ithaca: Cornell University Press, 2008.

Sears, Stephen W. *Gettysburg.* Boston: Houghton Mifflin, 2003.

Steele. *Civil War Atlas to Accompany Steele's American Campaigns.* Prepared by the department of civil and military engineering, United States Military Academy, for its course in military history. No publishing information given but was used by a member of the class in 1943.

Sword, Wiley. *The Confederacy's Last Hurrah.* Lawrence: University Press of Kansas, 1992.

Taylor, Alan. *American Colonies: The Settling of North America.* New York: Penguin Books, 2001.

Tucker, Glenn. *Chickamauga: Bloody Battle in the West.* Dayton: Morningside, 1992.

Time-Life Books eds. *Atlanta: Voices of the Civil War.* Alexandria: Time-Life Books, 1996.

Time-Life Books, eds. *Illustrated Atlas of the Civil War.* Alexandria: Time-Life Books, 1998.

Virginia Military Institute Archives, "The Funeral of Robert E. Lee," William Nalle letter. www.vmi.edu/archiv.

Weitz, Mark A. *More Damning than Slaughter: Desertion in the Confederate Army.* Lincoln: University of Nebraska Press, 2005.

Wilentz, Sean. *The Rise of American Democracy: Jefferson to Lincoln.* New York: W. W. Norton & Company, 2005.

www.jbhhs.com, website for the John Bell Hood Historical Society.

Zimmerman, Mark. *Guide to the Civil War Nashville.* Nashville: Battle of Nashville Preservation Society, 2004.

Made in the USA
Middletown, DE
27 December 2022

20478302R00087